A SOCIO-THEOLOGY OF LETTING GO

A SOCIO-THEOLOGY OF LETTING GO

The Role of a First World Church Facing Third World Peoples

by
Marie Augusta Neal, S.N.D. deN.

PAULIST PRESS
New York/Ramsey/Toronto

Library of Congress
Catalog Card Number: 76-50953

ISBN: 0-8091-2012-7

Published by Paulist Press
Editorial Office: 1865 Broadway, New York, N.Y. 10023
Business Office: 545 Island Road, Ramsey, N.J. 07446

Printed and bound in the
United States of America

ACKNOWLEDGMENTS

We herein express our gratitude to the following publishers for their kind permission to quote from the cited works:

The New York Times, for material attributed to that newspaper in the text, © 1972/73/74 by The New York Times Company. Reprinted by permission.

Association for the Sociology of Religion, for excerpts from the author's article "How Prophecy Lives," in *Sociological Analysis* 1972, 33, 3:125-141. Reprinted by permission of the Association for the Sociology of Religion, Executive Secretary, Northern Illinois University, DeKalb, Illinois 60115. Membership or subscription is $15.00 per year.

The Seabury Press, Inc., for excerpts from the author's article "Civil Religion, Theology and Politics in America," from *America in Theological Perspective,* edited by Thomas M. McFadden. Copyright ©1976 by The Seabury Press, Inc. Used by permission of the publisher.

The Religious Education Association, for the author's article "Civil Religion and the Development of Peoples," reprinted from the May-June 1976 issue of *Religious Education* by permission of the publisher, The Religious Education Association, 409 Prospect St., New Haven, Conn. 06510. Membership or subscription available for $20.00 per year.

The Boston Globe, for excerpts from the cited article by Crocker Snow, Jr. in the edition of April 14, 1974. Reprinted by permission.

Contents

Preface

In the mid-1950's, while the Catholic Church was still deeply immersed in the life of local parishes, the local parishes had become functionally ineffective for ministry in the changing city. Already a new mode of Christianity was in the making. A number of events—the destruction of the Jews in Germany, the dropping of the atomic bomb on Hiroshima, the elimination of the opposition in the McCarthyist period—had taught us at some level of consciousness a terrible truth: that we as a people were capable in our national systems of selecting a population for elimination, and that we could find the will to carry out that elimination by justifying it in a religious context.

It took the American Black to call on Christians to witness to the injustice of this anomaly—that, in the name of Christianity, we could both destroy and provide for life through the uses of religion and religious ministry. Caught up in slave roles at the beginning of the nation, Blacks were becoming sufficiently conscious both of the indignity of servile status and of the rights of people as human beings to share in the resources of the world into which all are born, and were beginning to organize and act in protest against the status accorded them. The civil rights movement was a prophetic movement, calling to account the American people whose faith, Sidney Ahlstrom records, was tested by this movement and by the end of the sixties found wanting.

Over the past ten years, groups of Christians reflecting on the conditions of our times have come increasingly to recognize the injustice of social structures which deny to the poor access to the resources that belong to them, and have sought ways to change those structures. The task, however, is more global now, as peoples rise up all over the world and, experiencing new life, reach out to claim their share of it. Color and race proclaim the

1

catholicity of the movement, even as the church gets caught up into national priorities. We pull back from the task into the security of the local community, following the rhythm of popular trends, while a growing apartheid at home and abroad witnesses to a more profound and serious need—to implement the Gospel's universality.

There are now four billion people in our world. From the point of view of Christianity—founded as an artisans' religion—priority belongs to the poor. So attractive is Christianity, however, that the rich are constantly reinterpreting it in order to make it speak for their interests. Whenever this happens in the course of history, the practice of Christianity loses its prophetic quality—that is, its capacity to call to account those who are exploiting the poor in their own interests—and becomes merely a rationalization of the status quo.

The church is called upon to support the poor as they reach out to take what is rightfully theirs. Currently the theology of liberation provides a method for the poor to reflect on their condition and, in response to the Gospel mandate, to transform the world. But, if their response is to be equally Christian, the rich need a theology too—for reflecting on what to do when they feel the touch of the poor. Traveling back and forth over the Charles River for the past three years—between Boston and Cambridge, Emmanuel and Harvard—to teach where caring people study the city from two very different perspectives has helped me to realize that a theology of liberation without a theology of relinquishment cannot touch us where we live and work, and so can change neither our lives nor the world in which we struggle. These essays consider the conditions of our society that call for a Christian response from the church. They invite the theologian to reflect and act with the people to shape such a response and to support it. They call for a theology of relinquishiment, where relinquishment refers not to symbolic private acts but to public initiatives in the form of debt moratoria and the release of resources.

There are many to whom thanks are due for reading and criticizing these essays. Special thanks to Ronald Marstin without whose constant editing assistance in the past three years few papers would have been ready for use at the event for which they were intended; to Mary Daniel, Marlene, Helen, Jeanne, my family and the women at Harvard Divinity School, for specific dialogue and reaction; to those colleagues, students and teachers alike, whose ideas have inspired my response and who have responded to my ideas; to the poor of the world, whose access to the resources they need is my primary concern and whose courage in acting when they see what needs to be done is my inspiration; to the Spring Street and Roxbury Sisters whose vision provides the dialectic; and to Emmanuel College, for the research-teaching appointment which provides the time to write while I continue the teaching that I love to do, in a setting that is both struggle and hope. But the book is dedicated to those sisters who provide the community that sustains my life as I work—Grace, Esther, Mary T. and Claudia—for without their presence and response there would be no life in which to work.

Emmanuel College
Boston, Massachusetts
April 1, 1976

A Reflection on
Leviticus 25:1-28*

Depending on our way of defining the world, we choose our strategy for making choices within it. First, if we perceive it to be all right the way it is—that is, if it is all right for us and not too threatening to our political, economic and social class interests—we act to preserve it. Our concern may very well be that people become holy, but holy will mean living in harmony. Second, if we perceive the world as needing reform, we will strive through educational, religious and recreational programs and models so to change the consciousness of the people that the system will work differently. Our definition of the holy will include outreach. Third, if we perceive that the world's interlocking systems have outlived their usefulness as channels of human energy toward human development, then we will no longer be able to exert our energies in the direction of social control or social reform but only, if at all, in the direction of social change. We will do this when we discover that, by keeping the rules we have devised, people suffer. Then the response of our minds and bodies to the advertisement of goods and services, to education, to recreation and religion—that is, to the celebration of life in this society—will be anomie and apathy. We will be ready to relinquish our hold on the system. When the poor reach out for what is theirs, we will be less likely to resist. We will wrestle with the holy. And fourth, if we are poor and we are encouraged to bond with our poor neighbors, we will grow in hope and in the courage to reach out to take what is ours for growth and development, rejoicing that God is at our

*During the teaching term, the chaplain at Harvard University customarily asks different members of the faculty to give short talks at daily morning prayer in Appleton Chapel. This one was given on March 1, 1974.

side sustaining our life and supporting our efforts. We will become the holy people.

It makes all the difference in the world which way we define the situation. Every choice we make of where we live, with whom we associate, what work we do, what courses we take or give, how we celebrate life and how we think, is made in the context of the way we define the social situation. For decades our universities taught as a liberating art a specific direction of economic development, with alternate forms defined as deviant. This does not necessarily define the university as subversive of liberal education but merely as a formal structure of the society it affirms, the society our churches celebrate.

When, however, two-thirds of the world live below the level of subsistence in order to keep this social system continuing in the direction for which it is structured, then somewhere in that society people who are not advantaged by the structures of the society must have space to develop alternate forms of social structure, deliberating together on human need as they experience it. Theologies of liberation direct the Gospel meditation to that end. But while those whose interests are not served by the existing system are so deliberating, and being affirmed and guided by the sacred Word, what should they be doing who are advantaged by the existing system? Perhaps developing a theology of "letting go." Accordingly, when the two-thirds of the world not advantaged by the system as it now exists reach out for what is theirs, those who have a firm grip on it (upon far more than they need to be humanly satisfied) will release their grasp rather than continue to blame the victims of the present inadequate structures for the conditions which they experience in their lives.

To do *this* theology we need to study the same disciplines we now study but from a somewhat different perspective. We need to study what is philosophically, theologically, scientifically, artistically and humanistically institutionalized, to determine how we can let it go. Then the human energy used up in retaining it can be released for transforming it, without destroying the people for whom the world exists.

Who are the people? To whom does the land belong? To

answer these questions the jubilee was instituted. Leviticus directs that we celebrate the jubilee every fifty years because in about that much time (given our human potential as now structured) we will have invented ways of wresting the land from the people and using it again to our own advantage. Scripture tells us to give it back to the widows and the orphans. According to the commentary, "it is the universal opinion of exegetes that this law represents an ideal rather than a practical law" (McKenzie, 1968, 460). What a glorious task for our time: to make the ideal a reality. Taking and letting go—this dialectic of human interaction is long out of practice because we have as yet no ethic to guide the process. But the people are awakening, and interaction is beginning. If we listen we can hear them singing and see them dancing and someday we can join them when they reach out to us, for God is with them, with the people.

1
Rationalization or Religion: When Is Civil Religion Not Religion but Merely Civil?*

Emile Durkheim described religion as "a system of ideas with which the individuals represent to themselves the society of which they are members, and the obscure but intimate relations which they have with it." "This," he said, "is its primary function" (Durkheim, 1965, 257). The proposition embodied in this observation and in the accompanying analysis is that the God most people worship is nothing more than "the collective and anonymous force of the clan," in other words, the social forces that bear upon people and that each one experiences both as coercive and compelling. "In a general way," Durkheim says at another point, "it is unquestionable that a society has all that is necessary to arouse the sensation of the divine in minds, merely by the power it has over them; for its members, it is what a god is to his worshippers" (Durkheim, 1965, 236). Durkheim's material on the elementary forms of religious life, and especially his quite explicit suggestion that religion might be explained completely by social forces, press the sociologist to examine carefully the relationship between church and society (Durkheim, 1965, 477).

In 1966, Robert Bellah applied to certain moral forces in society the term "civil religion" (Bellah, 1970, 168-186). For a decade his essay provided leverage for a spate of sociological research. Some current phenomena suggest the need for further examination in the 1970's of the intricate relationship between

*Paper given at the annual meeting of the Society for the Scientific Study of Religion, Washington, D.C., October 25, 1974.

religion and society. These include: the multiplication of religious forms, the shift in the stands of the conservative, liberal and radical churches in America, and the shift in a quite different direction of the churches at the international level. The alignment of church groups and church leaders with anti-government forces in Latin America and Africa, and recently in Spain and Portugal, suggests interesting changes in the societal identity that corresponds with religious commitment. These alignments further suggest differences in what can be called civil religion in developing as distinct from advanced technological societies.

In his essay, Bellah used Durkheim's analysis of the relationship of religion and society in proposing a paradigm for analyzing the national spirit. Without denying evidence of the exploitation of the powerless, Bellah recognized in the leadership of a nation the effective force of certain values—upheld by some leaders and affirmed by some citizens—that cut across gross class interest, extolling a quality of life such as to make membership in the nation something worth celebrating. He traced such an affirmation of quality in American life in the words and deeds of Lincoln, Kennedy and Johnson. His analysis was sufficiently persuasive at that time to encourage interest among denominational staff-people in a new study of religion and society and to prompt them to take the Hegelian risk—to trust that, whatever the present quality of national life, the Spirit was yet moving within society (Hegel, 1953). Given that assumption, there seemed reason for them to hope that support of the traditional national values in the congregational assembly would foster the realization of justice in public and private institutional role-sets as they now exist, and thus further humanize the people of the world—in which case the religious celebration of the nation would be justified. There is a risk, however, in this trust in the viability of the Spirit, for the priestly ministers enjoy no guarantee that the Spirit is in reality still with the nation. Unless, therefore, the ministers are able to test the spirit that moves them in their roles as leaders of the assembly, they may in effect—by reducing the guilt of the oppressor—simply be furnishing social cement for the preservation of the corporate state even if it is no longer structured in justice.

This discussion raises the question of what the spirit is, if anything, that moves a nation or any group to act as a body. Durkheim calls it a collective consciousness that makes of the members a moral whole (Durkheim, 1953, 169). He did not assume, as did Hegel, either that the spirit moved the whole world or that the spirit was rooted in reason. He did try to demonstrate, however, that what churches celebrate when the members gather for cultic action are the "obscure but intimate relations" between the members and the society of which they are members. By locating these relations in the psychic structures of the members, he leaves open the question of the class affiliation of church membership in pluralist societies, though what he says helps to explain the class association of churches. While Durkheim's focus was on primitive tribes, the object of his analysis was the modern nation.

Pursuing the Hegelian thesis, one can answer the question of this chapter by saying that religions that celebrate the nation in its current institutional form are no longer religious when two conditions obtain: (1) if the society is so structured in injustice that, by following the rules of the system, peoples suffer inhuman treatment; and (2) if the ministers of religion uncritically affirm this situation by taking a non-prophetic stand toward the society—by praying for the health of the rulers and giving thanks to God for life as it is lived within the society. Such a stance will alienate from institutional religions those oppressed peoples of the world who, as they become politically conscious, also become aware that, in its forms of law and order, the society is structured against their interests and in support of those who have power over them—in setting wages and prices, conditions of work, the limits of freedom of action, regulations for the use of societal resources, and so on. These people will be estranged from institutional religions to the extent that they realize that they have no real power to make their needs known or to claim that share of the commonwealth to which they are entitled either by citizenship or simply by their existence as human beings.

Such a non-prophetic stance will also lull into false consciousness the kept classes—that is, those who fulfill the service roles of the economy and polity. This is effected through the job orientation of the formal educational system, the release provided by the recreative institutions and the comfort provided by the institutionalized religions. These institutions socialize people into the culture as well as offer possibilities of reform. To the extent that they fail to take a prophetic stance toward an unjust society, they are party to the injustice. Simply put, then, in times of manifest injustice and in societies divided by class, the churches are called—through their normal functions of worship, service and community-making—to challenge rather than to comfort the powerful and kept classes and to identify sympathetically with the causes of the oppressed.

Where churches take up this prophetic task, new relationships with society develop. A prophetic stance in times of manifest social evil will generate discontent among church members when they feel themselves being comforted less than they have come to expect, and chided more; at least, that will be true where the congregation is predominantly of the powerful or kept classes. On the other hand, congregations that are predominantly of the oppressed classes will experience new joy and hope when, long accustomed to hearing an alien message from a clergy conditioned to uphold the status quo, they begin to hear the ministers—even in the context of worship and community-building—acknowledge their plight and support action to change it. While the clergy in such times will feel alienated from the advantaged classes, they will be reinforced in their roles by the poor. This reversal will effect changes in the quality of the services they provide, and consequently in the membership they serve and in the kind of people presenting themselves for ordination. Those changes will in turn generate the question of church support in the future, a question of money and of members (Pettigrew, 1959).

Some churches during the past two centuries have so identified with the social structure, that corporate sin is no longer a part of their repertoire of defined evil, personal salvation is defined as deliverance from an evil world, and personal counseling functions to adjust people to it. Consequently, their staffs have lost or have never developed any skill in reflecting on community reform, any radical critique of society or any adequate perception of the need for social change. At times in history calling for social restructuring, these church roles appear irrelevant. Especially is this so if the clergy continue to celebrate the old tradition which, in the course of reflection' by people within movements for social justice, is perceived as part of the evil structure and so stands condemned. That the religious system is judged irrelevant in the eyes of those who seek social reform reflects the fact that for them it has become merely civil. The clergy and other church members who remain faithful to the faithless social structure while the Spirit moves on (finding expression in social movements and in the Church-as-movement) will experience anomie; while the oppressed, becoming conscious of their oppression, and the advocates of a new society, lacking an adequately oriented religious leadership, will turn elsewhere for spiritual support.

This analysis assumes, of course, that the quality called Spirit by Hegel, by theologians, by religious people and social analysts is the same Spirit that Bellah examines in "Civil Religion in America." Pursuing the discussion with this assumption, we come to the question of whether there is any way to determine when the times call for a de-emphasis on the priestly function and a central emphasis on the prophetic. Is there any way to determine when it is incumbent on religious role players to dissociate their functions from the civil system? Can we know when continuing the union of God and country reinforces exploitation of the people? Can we know when religion should loosen the emotional attachment of the people from the status quo, the church becoming more movement than institution (Baum, 1968)? There seems to be evidence that the institutions of a society as currently structured in law and custom are unable to fulfill the functions that their names define as their purpose; when the agencies for health, education and welfare, for example, do not provide health, education and welfare for people lacking these services but do provide them for people who already have more than their share of them. That is one measure. Another would be when following the law prevents such action as would render society safe for its members; when the lawmakers resist change in those laws because what they and the interest groups they represent want is a body of law designed not to provide a safe society for the citizens but to protect their own private interests, interests which are at odds with those of the people for whom society should be providing. Or again, when medical services, although highly advanced in their potential for preserving life, are so costly that only the rich can freely choose to use them; and when those who provide the services resist programs that would give priority to the ill rather than priority to those who can afford to pay for medical care. Further, if there is evidence of a need for correctional reform because prisons not only do not rehabilitate but in fact generate recidivism; and when there is evidence that this is a function not of personal criminal acts but of the division of the common wealth to the advantage of those who invest over those who produce. Further evidence of structured evil is present if welfare services for the aged, the young, the disabled and the uneducated are made contingent on job performance when those in these conditions cannot work; when the racially and/or ethnically different are categorically excluded from preferred jobs, being given priority in job training for menial tasks, while job training for preferred tasks is allocated according to family membership rather than training need; if the laws and customs provide differential application of justice on the basis of ability to pay, or residence area; when access to these qualifications is withheld from segments of the population for reasons of bio-structure, cultural differences or zoning area. Evidence of structured evil obtains if poorly made goods and services are produced for purchase by the poor at prices higher than those of well-made goods for the non-poor (Walter, 1973); if more money is spent by the powerful nations for weapons to destroy people than for services for people's needs; if the people against whom the weapons are used are the poor and powerless nations whose natural resources, needed for the further development of the wealthy nations, are being bargained for as the people are being destroyed; if health and disaster services are withheld from whole nations and subcontinents of needy people in time of disaster because the territory is valueless. In all these instances, there is manifest evidence of societal action against the people and in the interests of advantaged classes. If at such times religions remain indifferent to those events, or celebrate the systems that generate them or, having means of aid, respond inadequately to them, then such religions have become merely civil or something close to it.

If these and other factors present in determining the rules and regulations of life in society are systematically withheld from examination in the schools or from being presented in the mass media, then religion *qua* religion is faced with the task of proclaiming the injustice and marshaling psychic energy for its redress. Through the church's worship, service and community development, the people decathect the unjust systems and build the new society in the interests of the oppressed. Religions that repudiate this task, set it aside as peripheral to their purpose or fail to recognize its existence, while at the same time they function to comfort the powerful and kept classes, assist in the maintenance of the unjust system. Such religions are thereby not religious but merely civil.

Machiavelli counseled princes to foster religion because a religious people is a docile people (Machiavelli, 1953). In the creation and maintenance of a just society, docility to a shared ideal can be a religious virtue. Priestly functions include celebrating life in such a society, in order to help people overcome the personal disaffections generated by inter-personal conflicts and feelings of inadequacy, and so to enable them to continue investing their energies in the just social system. But when the clergy and their celebrating communities continue these functions of personal adaptation and social affirmation in the unjust society, then in their acts of worship, service and community-making they have become merely civil and no longer religious.

One might want to ask at this point whether it is possible to become merely religious and not civil. This raises the whole question of the relationship between religion and society that Durkheim considers in *The Elementary Forms of the Religious Life.* Communal worship, he suggests, is by its very communality always creating and maintaining social order of some sort. Civil order affirms the existing political, economic and social structure. Religion either affirms this order or assists in reforming it. When the worshiping community passes judgment on the limitations of societal structures as no longer functional for fostering psychic survival for the peoples within the society, it engages by that act in the process of decathecting the system. Therefore, when at a given moment the gathered community finds no place on earth which is just and has only its ideal model in which to place its hope of salvation, then—for that group, at that moment—religion is purely religious and not civil at all. This is probably the reason that groups which withdraw from society and live apart feel more holy than the rest of society, why oppressed classes seek a purely other-worldly salvation in a heavenly city beyond time (Weber, 1963, 95-117), and why classes with power insist that religious role-players—if they want to keep their tax-free status—either stay out of politics entirely or else affirm as holy the society sustained by the powerful.

The fact remains that realizing the just society on earth is the central function of religious systems, and that function is constantly being co-opted to the function—not always recognized as distinct—of legitimating the status quo. How the religion realizes this function of creating the just society is historically specific. It is linked to the concept of God or the other ways, peculiar to each religion, of symbolizing the relation of human beings to the Spirit, analysis of which is the province not of sociology but of theology. Models for restructuring society will be developed by people alienated from the existing system in various ways. While their creative energy might be released by religious expression from attachment to the existing structures, it will be directed by their understanding of social process and by their political and economic experience.

The main functions of religious systems during periods of decathexis of the unjust society continue to be worship, service and community-development. What changes during such periods is the orientation of the religious expression. Instead of celebrating the injustices institutionalized in the existing political, economic and social order, religious expression takes the form of prophecy, which is the act of calling a nation to account for its exploitation of the people, and the discernment of spirits, which is declaring true the spirit that moves the prophet and those who respond to the prophet. These prophetic and discerning functions are just as subject to co-optation by established powers as are the priestly functions. A way is needed, therefore, to distinguish false prophecy and false discernment from the true functions. The true functions effectively address the problems of the oppressed peoples, which suggests a test of the truth of prophecy and discernment—in whose interest is it done? If, once the existence of an injustice has been recognized and addressed, there is affirmed a process of prophecy and discernment consistently pleasing to the established powers, while the prophecy and discernment recognized as helpful by the oppressed is put down, then it is fairly certain that the terms of the process have been co-opted to established interests. This is what happened, for example, with the "Great Society," "Manifest Destiny," "The New Frontier," "The Poverty Program and Compensatory Education," and the "Welfare State" (Piven, 1971). The list of abortive efforts at social reform suggests, in retrospect, that the essential to the radical restructuring of society lies in focusing meditation and reflection on the issues before and after action is taken.

Religious renewal presupposes the human proclivity to sin, but in periods of rapid social change the focus of this renewal needs to be more social than personal, and the object of renewal the evil propensities of the state rather than those of the person. At times when social stability is unjust, it is their failure to exert pressure on the social structure that characterizes religions as merely civil. At such times, focus on personal sin becomes "blaming the victim" (Ryan, 1970). The worship, service and community-making functions of religion remain central; changing social patterns, however, necessitate in the church an emphasis alternating between priestly and prophetic functions, between comfort and challenge. When society is structured in justice, religious celebration facilitates the channeling of human energy into fulfilling the roles needed to ensure societal continuation; when structured in injustice, religious celebration facilitates the decathection of the system. A religion that misses the transition becomes by that fact merely civil and not religious. In other words, it becomes a mere rationalization of the status quo. It was their observation of institutions of this type that led Marx to call religion the opium of the people and Freud to characterize God as a projection of the superego. Both were observing people in the society of their day and were ironically providing the prophetic function by their critiques of their society. Their secular critique of the religious factor paved the way for the proliferation of religious experimentation characteristic of the 1970's, as well as for the speculative reflection on the God problem in the 1960's.

Sources of Change Calling for Prophecy

It is an assumption of this chapter that the factors generating rapid social change appear at a more or less accelerated rate depending on their base or origin, a base constituted primarily by (1) population characteristics—for example, size and ethnic distribution, (2) the natural resources for survival, (3) the modes of their production and distribution and, only then, (4) the social, psychological and cultural structures developed to interpret these factors. Getting food, clothing and shelter sufficient for the survival of people is the foundation on which cultures develop, and change in any of these elements generates the need for basic structural changes in the economic and political order. The forms the structural changes take, however, are determined by the inventions of people in responding to the elemental changes. People do not respond to a valueless dynamic of population size, technological form or environmental condition, but to some policy programmed by those with the power to make decisions about how to deal with the changed conditions, a policy reflecting the perspective of the decision-makers. Accordingly, only when all the people participate in the making of decisions will the decisions be made in their interest. For no person can stand where another is except vicariously—after the other speaks his or her truth and the one is open to hear it. An unspoken position is an unknown variable. We have learned from social and psychological studies, however, and especially from the study of language and non-verbal communication, that people can define the situation for others, who then learn these definitions and take them as given, until something happens that raises questions about their absoluteness and provides for the examination of alternatives (Marx, 1959, 246-261; Douglas, 1972, 91).

In this frame of reference, movements express and bear witness to injustice felt by the movers and witnessed by their acts. The movements of the past twenty years include movements by racially different people for civil rights; by racially different nations for peace and justice; by students for freedom of speech and for structures enabling people to participate in decisions about the educational institutions which will shape their future; by Third World people for the right to make decisions about the disposal of mineral resources, arable land and energy resources in the lands where they reside; by colonized peoples, for redress of their grievances about cultural destruction; and currently by women for elimination of sexism in the home and in professional work roles. These movements have in common: (1) perceived injustices on the part of the people who experience the injustice, (2) people speaking on their own behalf, and (3) demands for return of property and rights on the basis of a new awareness of human communality and historical discrimination. Constantly, these movements are subject to exploitation by powerful interest groups and falsified in media presentations, but the growing consciousness of techniques of repression has already provided repressed groups with a measure of cultural power based on social awareness.

Factors causing an increased awareness of injustice in recent years include: (1) the fact that base population has so increased that zero population growth is seen as a value by those with advantage, but as certain subversion by those who have only their numbers to rely on in achieving the social structural changes they need if they are to acquire the power they see as essential to their development as a people; (2) technological development that calls for the restructuring of societies for the effective use of new modes of production and distribution of goods and services such as electronic-cybernetic systems; and

(3) the destruction of the environment, through the depletion of resources and the disposal of the waste products of industry. What these developments call for is a more rational use of natural resources—assisted by production designs geared to permanent and effective use rather than planned obsolescence—and a fairer distribution of goods. This in turn calls for popular control of international resources and markets, through popular participation in decision-making structures. Presently, decisions regarding the use of resources serve the interests of a minority and threaten the existence of two-thirds of the world's people. The rapidity of the changes is not the cause—contrary to the thesis of *Future Shock,* itself an example of conditioning to false consciousness—but rather the course of the policy programmed for the future by those who control the resources. The main injustice lies in the fact that the producers who have the power to make decisions about resources, and who are making decisions against the interests of the peoples whose resources they are disposing of, at the same time control the channels of information and interpretation of their decisions.

When conditions like this obtain and an established religion treats them as non-existent and of no concern of "ours," or as too enormous for us to contend with, or gives priority to other programs and themes, then the religion has become merely civil and not religious. Because truly religious activities or worship, service and community-making are oriented to the process of humanization, a test of the truth of priestly and prophetic functions can be found in the level of human development attained by peoples, having regard for the existing potential for human development. Religious exhortation of people to raise their minds and hearts "above bread-and-butter concerns" and to focus on "the aspirations of the human soul" and on promises of "salvation beyond the frustrations of human finitude," and the promotion of a "purely spiritual" salvation—such emphasis should be recognized as the class-conditioned values of the affluent for whom physical subsistence is no longer problematic. The poor are not naive in dreaming of a heaven that is quite material, which accurately reflects where they actually stand in the order of humanization. For them, any other aspiration would be irrational, not spiritual (Weber, 1963, 80-151). Established religions in affluent societies that have not recognized this fact or, having recognized it, still opt for the "purely spiritual" function are merely civil; for such an option, though it provides for the powerful and kept classes, is exploitative of the poor.

How does the social scientist demonstrate the distinction between the merely civil and the religious dimension of civil religion? After the fact, historical researchers do this by the analysis of history in cultural perspective. It is the task of the sociologists and social psychologists to seek to determine what expressions of religious belief are equated with what attitudes toward oppressed people as well as what follows from this equation. If—in a world in which unjust conditions are in fact manifest—a distinction is demonstrated between, on the one hand, a religious practice significantly related to the denial of such conditions and, on the other, a religious practice related to the recognition of such conditions, and if there exists a high probability that the relationships are not spurious or the result of chance, then there is reason to believe that religious practice closely tied to the maintenance of existing social arrangements is merely civil. Given, among other problems, those of false prophecy and false discernment mentioned earlier, the social scientist must proceed with great caution; but what ought not to continue is the current naive assumption that any sociological analysis that stands against the status quo is merely political action, and that which accepts it uncritically (or even critically) is neutral or objective. This distinction is a guide so long as injustice is rampant within the system. To date, sociologists have developed far better methods to explain and even justify existing relationships between institutions in society than they have done to demonstrate how those relationships effectively change or under what conditions they should change, given a change in their originally intended functions.

Evidence that the link between religion and society is part of the common understanding of people can be seen in the very way conditions of religion in society are reported. In *The New York Times* of April 14, 1974, Hedrick Smith reported, in an article entitled "Religion Is Still Deeply Embedded in Soviet Society":

> By and large the Orthodox hierarchy, traditionally a conservative force, has avoided clashes with secular authority —much as it did under the czars. Patriarch Pimen and other leaders give sermons endorsing or praising social and political policies, and they have defended the Soviet government against accusations from abroad of suppression of religion and civil rights.

Further in the same article, Mr. Smith continues:

> They want to represent the Church as the guardian of the 'National Spirit' eternal for all times (p. 26).

Given the definition of the Soviet system as civilly atheistic, this activity on the part of the Russian Orthodox Church is puzzling from a religious perspective if one misses the point that religions express the "obscure but intimate relations" individuals have with their society. The increasing dialogue today between Christians and communists begins to make clearer to us as observers of our times that the categorical rejection of religion expressed by Karl Marx, juxtaposed with his clearly service orientation to the working class and his concern for the "lumpen proletariat" (the as yet unaware masses who tend to celebrate in religious context the unjust society that oppresses them), was not a philosophical but an historical stance, a response to the conditions of his time—a time in which the churches were more civil than religious and the society manifestly unjust.

In 1973, reporting in *The New York Times* on the current situation in the Philippines in an article entitled "Church in Philippines Becoming a Focus of Opposition to Marcos," Joseph Lelyoeld wrote:

> To the consternation of many conservative bishops, the

Roman Catholic Church is becoming an increasingly important focus of resistance to the martial-law government of President Ferdinand E. Marcos.

In its most extreme form this resistance is expressed in support for programs of armed revolution including that of a Communist underground that takes its inspiration from the Chinese leader Chairman Mao Tse-tung. A handful of priests and young Catholic laymen have actually joined the Communists. Others, belonging to a group called Christians for National Liberation, are said to be planning guerrilla activities of their own.

The government has reacted by viewing social action programs of the church on behalf of peasants, plantation workers and urban squatter colonies as potential sources of subversion. Churches and convents have been raided by military units and a few priests and nuns detained for interrogation. . . .

(The government's) concern is easily explained. Nearly 85% of the Filipinos identify themselves as Catholics. The church has not taken a united stand on secular issues since Spanish colonial rule ended in 1898, but if it ever did it would obviously be a formidable force.

"We have been telling the bishops, 'Please tell the members of the clergy not to rock the boat,'" the Secretary of Defense, Juan Ponce Enrile declared in an interview. A large number of young priests, nuns and seminarians here are familiar with the radical writings of church thinkers in other parts of the world, especially Latin America. "The Theology of Liberation" by Gustavo Gutierrez, a Cuban (sic), is now being widely circulated.

"The Pedagogy of the Oppressed" by Paulo Freire had a sale of 3,000 copies, almost entirely to priests, nuns and seminarians (October 18, 1973, p. 3).

This article provides a proposal for testing the thesis that civil religion can be merely civil and not religious. It calls for an examination of the actions taken by religious role players in the Philippines, of the behavior of the hierarchy, the clergy, the members of religious orders and the local peoples, as they perform acts of worship, ministry and community development during this period of threat to the social structures of the island caught up in the traid-aid interests of powerful economic forces. The island has an 85% Catholic population, with a large repressed Muslim minority now identifying with Chinese mainlanders, but it also has a peasantry awakening to political consciousness. *The Boston Globe* cites a relevant article on April 14, 1974, entitled "Philippine Priests Using Easter Sermons To Condemn Martial Law." The paper's Asian correspondent Crocker Snow, Jr. reported in part:

> The issue of the political activism of the church has been a sensitive one since martial law was first declared by President Marcos in September, 1972, all allegedly because of a serious threat to the government by "Maoists."

> The clampdown came less than two years after Pope Paul VI visited Manila and joined all Asian bishops in a joint resolve "to speak out for the rights of the disadvantaged and powerless" and to "not tie our hands by compromising entanglements with the rich and powerful". . . .

> This open opposition by a small activist element within the church has led to veiled threats from President Marcos beginning last fall that the "privileges of the pulpit" as a political and tax-free sanctuary could be lost forever.

> Church sources report that this threat hangs "like a sword of Damocles" over the most conservative Catholic elders who control large land-holdings in the central island of Luzon. . . .

A Spanish priest on the island is recorded as saying:

> "It is the position of the church to proclaim the Gospel

with the stress on peace and justice. In so doing we must challenge the government as it is today. It's inevitable."

The content of this article provides descriptions of three directions of response taken in a religious context—conservative, liberal and radical:

> The most cautious feel that it is important for them to avoid confrontation with the government as the best way to administer to the people's needs (Conservative).

> Others, like the country's senior churchman, Archbishop Jaime L. Sin of Manila, represent a middle road, treading a careful course between the liberal and conservative winds of the clergy (Liberal).

> [In response to the actions] of Father Luis Jalandoni, picked up carrying a .38 revolver and the writings of Mao Tse-tung, a little-publicized statement of support was written by a group of fellow-priests: "No one can deny that Father Luis tried all means then on hand—the law, the courts, the bureaucracies, the pulpit, persuasion and diplomacy, personal contacts and influence, even pressure methods like strikes and demonstrations," they said (Radical).

These familiar-sounding quotations constitute the categories into which we place response to political action of an authoritative sort by the churches. We learn from these reports that religious fervor, commitment and belief are elements of a person's religion that energize the person to act with, on or against social systems, and that all three positions can have a genuine link with the religious dimension and the political scene. Research monographs that have examined religion in America in the past twenty years—Pettigrew and Campbell's *Religion in Racial Crisis*, Lenski's *The Religious Factor*, Glock and Stark's *Religion and Society in Tension*, Greeley's studies of parochial schools and Catholic priests, Herberg's *Protestant, Catholic, Jew* and my own *Values and Interests in Social Change*, among others—give evidence that the official churches at the national and international levels have been clearer and stronger in their statements of the centrality of action for social justice as a religious responsibility than have the local parishioners in their behavior or the local clergy in their expectations. At the local level, Gordon Allport's assessment of the 1950's still holds true —namely, that the parish is often "an island of safety" for its members; or, in Glock's categories of religious action, "to comfort" is a higher expectation for church members than "to challenge."

The studies of the same type in the early 1970's show a return to this mentality after the liberal stirrings of the late 1960's. Jeffrey Hadden foretold this return to the "comfort" theme in the late 1960's in *The Gathering Storm in the Churches;* David Moberg's *The Great Reversal* pointed to the trend among evangelicals; Dean Kelly pointed to it among Protestant churches in general in *Why the Conservative Churches are Growing;* and finally, Andrew Greeley advocates it in *The Denominational Society.* Each of these books shows not only the local middle class churches celebrating their own life and grieving over their identity problems, but later reacting strongly against the introduction of a more critical stance on the part of the church toward the injustices in the formal structures of the society. Disruption of the church is threatened in the form of withdrawal of money and members. The manifest target is the loose morality tolerated by the liberal church, but attitudes ranging from relative indifference to outright resistance to the demands of the poor suggest a siege mentality and an intended co-optation of the church to protect those inside the walls— where the walls, be they in the city, suburb or countryside, exclude the two-thirds of the world who live below subsistence level. Pettigrew and Campbell concluded in 1957 that, despite the ardent dedication of some clergy and laity, the fear of loss of money and members would in fact in the long run determine the decision of the majority of the local clergy to return to their communal role of comforting, even though the challenge of injustice still obtained in the society and called for a response from the churches. It is hard to say whether this behavior is totally civil and not religious, but the evidence of the decades fairly well substantiates that religious activity that goes on at the local level, where it ignores the cry of third world people, is a compromise of the central commitment of religions to the development of peoples beyond class interest, no matter how real is the anguish of the powerful or kept classes.

As long as the local church so resists, the proclamations of the national churches are ineffective platitudes even when liberal in form. A radical stance alone will provide for social change. In Latin America, the decisions of the bishops' conference at Medellin in 1968 legitimated clergy- and lay-participation in subversive activity against intransigent and unjust social structures and in movements for liberation of the poor. One could say that from that time forward the conservative churches began to become merely civil and not religious to the degree that they have ignored or resisted this mandate. Reporting for *The New York Times* on July 27, 1972, Joseph Novitski states:

> Brazil's Roman Catholic bishops in the last two months have begun to stake out a clear position as defenders of the little man and champions of human rights in a country where varying degrees of repression are the rule.

In the summer of 1973, documents prepared by some of the bishops of the northeast were withdrawn from public circulation by government order. One of these, entitled "I Hear the Cries of My People," states in part:

> Before the suffering of our people, humbled and oppressed for centuries, we feel called by the Word of God to take up a position, a clear position on the side of the poor, a position taken in common with all those who commit themselves to the people for their true liberation (Brazilian Bishops, 1973).

Once established religions take an unambiguous stand with the poor, the long-standing harmony between church and state breaks down, no matter how characteristic it has been in the past. In Spain, for example, despite the fact that the Catholic Church officially scandalized itself during the Civil War in the 1930's by standing with the oppressive regime against the working class effort at self-liberation, when it speaks out today for the poor the government steps in immediately to condemn and threaten withdrawal of financial and public support. This is evident in *The New York Times* report entitled "Spain Is Said To Threaten End of Pact with Vatican":

> Madrid, March 7, 1974. The threat to end the Concordat, a treaty with the Vatican that since 1053 has conferred great privileges on the Spanish clergy, was believed to have been made last night by Premier Carlos Arias Navarro in a talk with the Primate of Spain and Archbishop of Toledo the Most Rev. Marcelo Gonzales Martin. . . . Under the Concordat, churchmen are exempt from military service, church property is inviolate and tax exempt, churchmen sit on most of the high panels of the state and the teaching of the Catholic religion is obligatory in all schools. A church prelate receives a monthly stipend from the government which also spends millions of dollars annually to subsidize religious schools and social centers run by the church as well as to maintain church buildings.

The cause of this threatened withdrawal:

> . . . the refusal of Bishop Antonio Anoveros Ataun of Bilbao to leave the country after he was sanctioned for authorizing the reading in the churches of his diocese of a homily upholding the right of the Basques to keep their identity in the use of their language, etc. (March 7, 1974).

In the following month, this report came from Portugal regarding guerrilla action in Mozambique:

> Adding to the government's problems is the opposition shown among members of the Roman Catholic Church in Mozambique. The Bishop of Nampula, the Most Rev.

Manuel Vieira Pinto, and his secretary, the Rev. Joa Cabral, were expelled early this week along with 11 missionaries . . . for criticizing the war and the Portuguese church hierarchy's attitude of subservience to the government (*The New York Times,* April 19, 1974, p. 9).

From Africa also came reports of dissociation of the civil from the religious institutions. *The Guardian* reported on April 5, 1974, with Henry Miller writing from Salisbury, Rhodesia:

The Rhodesian Minister of Justice, Law and Order, Mr. Desmond Lardner-Burke, today accused the country's Roman Catholic bishops of attempting to promote a Church-State confrontation and of trying to undermine law and order in Rhodesia. Speaking in the Senate, Mr. Lardner-Burke also obliquely linked the Roman Catholic Church here with the guerrilla cause.

The bishops of Rhodesia have criticized the existing Rhodesian government for its illegal assumption of office in 1965 and for the adoption of a Constitution on the basis of the voting white minority against the interests of the 95% black majority. The Land Tenure Act of 1971 which requires that the churches declare themselves for whites or blacks has been resisted, though timidly, by the churches. The timidity of this stance reflects the real pull on an established church either to celebrate the existing system and deny its own doctrine or to affirm its doctrine and risk legal action against it on the part of the civil authorities. The role of the church in Southern Africa is one of the clearest cases among modern nations of the contradiction within a religion between belief and expected practice, and for that reason is a test case for examining a whole range of religious-civil disharmonies in modern society and for refining the distinction between civil religion and religion (Moodie, 1975).

The argument that these examples are carry-overs from the old church-state relationship and do not parallel the relationship of the pluralist church denominations in the United States to civil systems is, I think, sociologically unsound. The sociologi-

cal literature continually documents an effective relationship between the pluralist church system in the United States and the
officially undefined class structure of American society. The
case remains strong that religious expression in modern society
fluctuates between being totally civil and radically salvational.
This does not mean the same thing as being totally turned toward this world and totally turned toward the other world; it
means, rather, totally reinforcing the unjust status quo and
being totally dedicated to changing it. The former analytic di-
chotomy moves from secular to religious, the latter from rationalization to religion. It is the latter type analysis that I think is
needed today and is being currently obscured by the secular-
sacred categories.

2
American Civil Religion and World Poverty*

On May 1, 1974, the sixth special session of the General Assembly of the United Nations adopted a Declaration and Program of Action regarding the problems of raw materials and development. It was entitled "Declaration on the Establishment of a New International Economic Order" (United Nations, 1974). It came at the end of a several-week period in which ninety-five of the developing nations of the world presented evidence of the needs of their people to participate in the decisions made about the disposal of the resources of their countries in production and trade in order for them to survive as human beings. For the poor of the world it was a great event: the first time representatives of that 70% of the world's population possessing only 30% of its income had occasion to stand up and claim what is theirs—namely, a human share in the planning and use of world resources. Having organized in order to have enough power to speak effectively, they stated clearly what were their basic needs in the social order in an emerging world society. The target of attack was the American-based multinational corporation, its European counterparts, and the governments that support them. Only six nations voted against that charter. One hundred and ten voted for it. Ten discreetly abstained because of the link of their immediate interests with the six vetoing nations. America vetoed, offering instead a proposal of aid

*Excerpted from "Civil Religion, Theology and Politics in America," a paper delivered at the plenary session of the Annual Convention of the College Theology Society, Boston College, May 30, 1975. Reprinted by permission of Seabury Press from *America in Theological Perspective* (New York: Seabury Press, 1976).

in time of disaster. Vietnam, Cambodia, Western Africa, Chile, Brazil, the Dominican Republic and Northern Ireland, as well as the Middle East, are examples of the kind of aid we are able and willing to provide to developing nations. These countries, long poor and used in the interests of non-residents, relate to America in a way similar to America's own inner-city areas, all being places where the expendable people live. Neither the United States nor South Africa has been able to finance free health care, education, and care for the elderly in all the years of affluence, yet China learned how to do it and to carry out what they learned for eight hundred million poor and alienated people in twenty-two years. The difference in performance is related to a difference in the perception of the worth of people. We learn our evaluations of people in our religious systems. They are informed by our theology.

In early January 1974, I met with an international organization of people involved in Christian communications media. Twenty-nine denominations, including the Catholic, were there. I asked them what coverage they gave to the sixth special session of the United Nations. They asked me to what event I was referring. A show of hands from the delegates revealed five who even knew it had occurred. How do we reflect theologically on the events of our times if we do not know what is going on? Journals and newspapers as well as the verbal and visual media are organized and staffed by those who share a certain vision of what is worth seeing and reflecting on. The daily press scarcely covered this event in the United States. China and Japan did cover it. If the religion is civil it is done in the interests of those whose interests are protected by the laws of the civil society. Our American conscience as shaped by our civil religion will hold in purview only those people we define as worthy to be viewed and it will do this according to our previous evaluation of who has the right to life and to the resources necessary to sustain that life. The poor are not central to that view (Piven, 1971; Magdoff, 1969; Greene, 1970).

Two-thirds of the world live below the level of subsistence in a world system which has technological potential for resolving this problem in the interests of all people. Nation-states have adopted an operating rule making international decisions in their own business interests even when such interests jeopardize the lives, the freedom and the development of the peoples over whom they have economic power, but to whom they have no citizen commitment by law. Some theologies affirm that rule. Some do not. There is a powerful movement in America and other first world countries to rest justice solely in entitlement. What the law defines as the rule of exchange then becomes the basis of justice, so that civil rights take precedence over human rights. A book propounding that rule won the religion and philosophy prize for 1975 in the national book awards in America—Robert Nozick's *Anarchy, State and Utopia* (New York: Basic Books, 1975). Exchange theory in sociology is becoming or has already become the most advocated form of sociological analysis on the university campus. It propounds similar standards for justice. In the words of George Homans:

> A man in an exchange relationship with another will expect that the rewards of each man be proportional to his costs—the greater the rewards the greater the costs—and that the net rewards, or profit, of each man be proportional to his investments—the greater the investments, the greater the profits (Homans, 1958).

If Leviticus 25:25-28 and Luke 3:7-11 represent our theological perspective on the social order, then the new international economic order, as well as concern to hasten the current activity toward a planned economy for the United States in the interest of people, will be central elements in our theological reflection on the jubilee, that is, on the biblical summons to return the land to the people. These would not be the central concerns for an American civil religion because the problem can only be solved in world perspective. Civil religion sets limits to the alternative social structures it can celebrate and still remain civil. From a sociological perspective it seems that at this time a world economy that honors the developing peoples and provides for the development of the peoples of the world stands outside what American society can affirm. It certainly stands outside

what America did in fact affirm regarding the United Nations'
economic charter.

The Hartford Statement (Hartford, 1975) gathered signa-
tures from American theologians who had become concerned
that God was no longer the center of theological reflection because theologians had become too absorbed in the social, economic and political order. I submit that the problems of the
social order in world perspective, that is, beyond the confines of
the civil perspective, have scarcely touched the vision of theology in America in a serious way—in such a way, that is, that
God-language might come to name a divine relationship with a
world society that goes beyond the interests of traditionally-
structured Western society. Since this traditional society is no
longer able to embrace the demands of the world's poor for
what they need for survival, though many of those poor live either within the confines of the traditional society or under its
control, then its theologies cannot reach to God, that is, they
cannot reach beyond the special interests of the advantaged in
the society in which they were developed.

Basil Moore and Sabelo Ntwasa, trying together to clarify
why the God of European theological reflection does no more
than reinforce Southern African white control over the black
population, say in part:

> In South Africa the Christian God's whiteness has been
> there from the beginning, if not always overtly. The strange
> white man arrived on our soil with his strange new God,
> and set himself up as the ecclesiastical authority—a posi-
> tion he has never relinquished.

Having questioned the usefulness of the emphasis on God-as-
person, given its sexual implications, they continue:

> Thus the symbol of God as 'Father' reinforces his maleness
> and authority; God as 'Son' reinforces his maleness; God
> as 'Shepherd' or 'Guide' or 'Lord' or 'King' or 'Master' re-
> inforces his authority; even God as 'servant,' like God as
> 'Father,' while attempting to express God's loving concern,

still carries strong overtones of authority (Moore, 1974, 23).

Authority is the presence of the oppressor in an apartheid society.

Mary Daly has made similar points from the perspective of women in America (Daly, 1973). The point is that language about God does not yet reveal space or hope for the oppressed peoples of the world. Because this is the case, theology is experienced by these oppressed peoples as a political act done in the interest of those whom the nations support, that is, the middle and upper classes, whites and males. For oppressed people words about God are merely another factor in the culture they experience as oppression, both within their countries and outside of it. For them, civil religion is not religious but merely civil.

The Societal Community

Prior to the current ascendancy of exchange theory in the academic community, structure-functional theory dominated sociological analysis. The current emphasis on exchange theory marks a shift in academic interest from the nation-state to the world trade system as the organizing principle of human intercourse. This shift to exchange theory is a basis of theological anxiety because it focuses the roots of world order in the international trading market and, in the development of international law, gives priority to the production and exchange of goods and services for development over human life and its development (Larson, 1973; Paul VI, 1967). That shift was the reason for my introducing for theological consideration the development and presentation of the United Nations' economic charter, a document and a program that would shift the emphasis of world order from the old affirmation of the trade elites to a new affirmation of all the peoples of the world. Exchange theory, as well as the newer sociobiology, furthers this elite trading interest, according to Edward O. Wilson, whose *Sociobiology: The New Synthesis* brings social Darwinism again to the fore with new prestige and interest.

Talcott Parsons has been the main exponent of structure-functional theory and his theory of social systems is the major theory of that school. In his most recent theoretical explication he defines a society as "that type of social system characterized by the highest level of self-sufficiency relative to its environment, including other social systems" (Parsons, 1971, 8). Then he proceeds to show how a society maintains itself in the self-sufficient state, through (1) the use of technology and an economy to exploit the physical environment, (2) the linking of the ecology to the division of labor by allocating economic interests among the various subgroupings of the population, (3) the political function, which means controlling action within the territory by the use of physical force (police and military) to prevent undesired action, (4) control of its membership by being able to count on the members to perform adequately the tasks needed for this self-sufficiency (rather than be alienated from the ways the institutions operate). This commitment of membership requires that the cultural system of the society be internalized in personalities, that the social system also be internalized, and that the cultural system be institutionalized in the social system. These tasks of conditioning human psychic energy to the performance of the jobs that need doing for a society to maintain its self-sufficiency bring us to the heart of the uses of sociology within a given society. (5) Finally, for self-sufficiency Parsons notes that the society's institutions must be legitimized in two ways: (a) by the values its members hold in common with relative consensus, and (b) by congruence with the other components of the cultural system and especially that component he calls the system of constitutive symbolism. Constitutive symbolism is the core of the religious system, he declares, and he ends his formula for self-sufficiency by noting that ultimately values are legitimized in religious terms (Parsons, 1971, 9).

Here, then, is the point of confrontation of the theologian and the sociologist. I fully realize that the last paragraph may be, from a theological perspective, boring and even meaningless but it is still, from a sociological perspective, the heart of the matter. What Parsons is saying is that unless a social geographical entity can be self-sufficient, as he defines self-sufficiency, it is not a society. Now, if you work back through his criteria, neither America, nor Germany, nor England, nor any other nation-state can by his criteria any longer be a society, because none is any longer self-sufficient in this sense. Once it uses its technology to control the resources of the world in its own interests, then a nation-state invades the socio-cultural systems that define other societies. If each is struggling to be self-sufficient in the sense defined here, then each is over-stepping the boundaries of the other. If, then, the religion that is operative in any one of these systems is maintaining the values that honor self-sufficiency as the yardstick of societal status for a rich nation-state, then the religion, along with the other institutional units of that so-called society, is acting against some people of the world in the interests of others.

This poses a problem for Christian theologians. Theoretically, Christianity stands with the poor of the world against all established interests that work to the manifest advantage of the rich man seeking to get through the eye of the needle. Historically, then, it should always be in judgmental tension with societal systems, especially as these systems have come in time to institutionalize the interests of advantaged segments of the society. Such, however, has not been the case. When Christianity remains true to its scriptural base, it is prophetic with respect to institutionalized exploitation. Membership, then, in organizations defined as Christian—that is, churches or mentalities that are distinctly Christian—should provide people with an affiliation alternate to their citizenship groups, in order to assure space for psychic solidarity that is not either easily co-opted into citizenship enthusiasm or repressed as defying the law. Civil religion as cultural enthusiasm and solidarity—by its very identification with established authority and even when it stands in criticism of that authority—collapses the social base for a prophetic stance. It also decreases the possibility of creativity in the expressive modes, having limited the basic assumptions about social structures from which ideas about changing those structures might develop. From this perspective it appears that civil religion reduces tension and in so doing provides for the experience of a pseudo divine assurance that the cultural norms associated with established power are closer to the will of God than is critical judgment passed on them, even when these cultural norms provide not for the life but for the death of the people. The idea of civil religion is popular today because, for any nation to assert its right to program the world economy in its interests, those in power need the assurance of a naive, spontaneous, uncritical, "religious" celebration—in Durkheim's term, an "effervescence"—to mask the mass exploitation that such a program requires. Religious enthusiasm uncritically expressed and charismatically released is one of the most effective ways of delaying the deluge.

Theologians are faced with a serious task in developing words about God that are as effective as those of other sciences when they categorize substance, matter and energy, mind and behavior, people by race and location, society and social systems, but that are not exploitative. If the sociologist discovers that there is now no society in our world because there is no self-sufficient geographical unit, that is, no people grouping in its own interests that does not by that very fact exploit other people whose interests are not its established concern and whose rights are not protected by its laws, then national gods become incredible. Language about gods corresponds to language about law, and both change as we become aware of other people whom we previously ignored. Down through history people have changed their perspective from household gods to tribal gods, from tribal gods to national gods, from national gods to class gods. Karl Marx challenged the classism of religion and Max Weber demonstrated its existence, as has the research of sociologists in America since Liston Pope named the denominations by class in 1948 (Pope, 1949). Today, American Blacks ask us, "Is God a white racist?" (Jones, 1973). The research of the 1960's on religion and prejudice, surveying the opinions of the majority of practicing Christians, suggests that the answer to that question is yes (Glock and Siegelman, 1969). Our cities overwhelmingly affirm that minister and people alike are still racist. Today, in pleading with us to move beyond partriarchy, women reach out for language about God that is non-familial;

and we scarcely hear their reasons because they come so close to our personal identities and private gods.

In a year when we are asked to deal with justice as a program of social action we can well recall the historical development according to which Roman law affirmed only the rights of household heads in its *paterfamilias*. The Middle Ages dealt with the divine right of kings, which Dante immortalized by locating in hell (in the perfect ordering of *The Divine Comedy*) the popes who challenged this divinity of kingly rights—though the political implications of this scarcely touch our consciences. Modern nations began their religious activity under the rule of *cuius regio, eius religio,* not under a people's choice. A concern for civil rights moved us to affirm in the 1950's that separate education is never equal. And today, human rights—affirmed by no law but stirring the new collective consciousness of a world of people newly aware of their own power and the processes of empowerment—seek a law, an ethic, a religious affirmation that our sciences have few words to name, a divine law neither modeled in the image of powerful civil systems nor proclaiming the same values, but standing in tension with such systems as it affirms the life of all peoples.

There was a time when civil religion was holy. This was during the period of the development of nations. It is still holy for developing peoples. But in America today it is a rationalization for the status quo—as the plight of our cities reveals only too painfully. American theologians, like all first world theologians, are called upon to develop a theology of relinquishment as the peoples of the world rise up to take what is rightfully theirs. For theologians, patriotism cannot be a primary virtue. Nation-states are today important societal units and nations are often cultural units that can and should celebrate their solidarity. However, if the God the advantaged people worship continues to be the society in which they live, then the anomie and alienation generated by disenchantment with an unjust social system will increase among the poor of the land. We can no longer afford to do theology—that is, to generate words about God—in any context which is less than global, or within the mental framework that defines peers as children, no matter who is called father. Transcendence, immanence and spirit need affirmation—but not in the language of family, community or society. God is not American no matter how much we would like this to be. Neither is God male, nor white, nor civil, nor economic, nor human. One cannot speak about God, however, without including these elements. What words, then, can we use to speak about God? That all depends on who the "we" are who do the speaking and for whom it is done. But from here on the problem is the theologian's, not the sociologist's. Politicians you will meet will try to convince you to unite as they try to bind together—*re-ligare*—the units in which they have power, so that they can control the reflection and enthusiasms of the people. For some, yes, God is society; for the theologian, that is at least a moot question. Listen to the speech of the people.

3
Civil Religion and the
Development of Peoples*

What has changed since Robert Bellah claimed in 1966 that "there exists alongside of and rather clearly differentiated from the churches an elaborate and well-institutionalized civil religion in America" (Bellah, 1970, p. 168) is the American experience itself. Sidney Ahlstrom defined that change in his succinct evaluation of the 1960's: "The American moral and religious tradition was tested in this decade and found wanting" (Ahlstrom, 1972, p. 1085). The test of our moral and religious tradition came in the form of the assertion of the rights of developing people to the resources they need for their survival, coupled with the resistance or refusal of America as a nation to loosen its grasp on these resources, even to the point of not according to revolutionaries the right to make their own revolution against those who held power over them—power they thought they ought to share. America could not *not* interfere in such nations as Chile, Cuba, Korea, Vietnam, Angola and Rhodesia, or in the lives of people asserting their rights in the inner city or on the university campus, because in a very real sense the destinies of all these people are tied up with the American national interest.

Given Parsons' analysis, outlined in the previous chapter, of what it takes to be a society, the members of no nation-state today, were they motivated by a religion claiming to be more than the worship of local gods, would want that state itself to be

*From a paper delivered at the plenary session of the International Convention of the Religious Education Association, Philadelphia, Pa., November 24, 1975, and published in the *Journal of Religious Education,* March-April, 1976.

a society. In the past, when people lived in tribes or even in city-states, it was functional to worship household gods, tribal gods or city gods, and the ancient Greeks and Romans founded their cities with such gods. The early peoples of biblical times vied with one another to test the power of their gods through their capacity to kill and to provide. From such a perspective, other peoples are not exploited because one knows that they too have their gods. We have long since opted, however, for an understanding of ultimate reality, if we are interested in such a reality, as one God. Granted that down through recent history we have also opted for seeing ourselves and our progeny as the elect of that God, missioned by God's command to bring salvation to the less fortunate, yet we now know that we are no longer able to do this nor is there any further need for us to do it as a chosen people. People are today rising up to claim their own rights. The task is to hear them and to take them seriously.

We now know that in carrying out what we saw as our mission we have not been able to define all people as people because we could not see the possibility of providing goods and services for any more than "our own." Given that limited vision, we affirmed philosophically, as a principle of governance, that we mandate our governors to make decisions in the common interest, where "in the common interest" meant in the interests of the nation's citizens. However, we proceeded to deprive of citizenship those who differed from us either in belief (the Quakers in Puritan New England, the Jews in Germany in the 1930's), or in status (the slaves in the nineteenth-century south and in the Greek city-states), or in color (the blacks in southern Africa today and blacks and ethnics in twentieth-century America), or in sex (women in all societies until they fought with their fists and fasted to death). In every case there was a violation of basic religious belief and yet a justification in terms of the same belief system. Such uses of religious belief disenchanted the workers of nineteenth-century Europe and today threaten the credibility of institutionalized religion in modern American society among youth, blacks and women. This is accompanied by the rise of disorder that Parsons' analysis points out will follow when the norms of society are not internalized in the psyches of the members.

Given a monotheistic conception of ultimate reality, and given what it takes to constitute a society, it would seem that it is time to consider a more radical separation of religion and state than that embodied in what we now call civil religion. We are being forced to become more aware of international interdependence for human resources. In our current limited conception of social systems, a conception limited not so much by our ignorance as by our historical experience, we have yet to try new modes of international law. Without connoting the construction of international states, such new modes of international law would need be inspired by religious conceptions more biblical than those presently in use, conceptions that would require calling to account the administrators of any nation, including our own, whenever they violate the rights of the people to health services, education, and welfare—conceptions that would affirm the right of people to participate in decisions about the uses of the land on which they reside, and the right to the land they need for their survival (Leviticus 25:1-28; Matthew 25:31-46; Miguez Bonino, 1975).

At present, our law systems, far from being called to account through our belief systems, are locked into the legitimization of our economies, economies themselves accountable to no moral or legal code except that which is made by the controllers (Brown, 1974). We deliberate in a religious context on whether we have violated the existing law, and perhaps urge atonement; we seldom deliberate in a religious setting on whether the existing law violates the standards of our religious systems. We often do not even know what these standards are, if indeed there are any (Glazer, 1972). A conception of law rooted in morality is constantly vitiated but we have no leverage for challenging the claimed relationship between the law and morality, so well have we taught ourselves that law and order are either not subject to religion or are by their very existence in harmony with it. I am not saying that we do not have scholarly treatises that address themselves to this task. We have many. I am saying that for religious educators to teach the skills needed for calling to account the functionaries of the government or of the economy for their exploitation of the people, and for providing reflective space for the people on every occasion to decide what to do in order to right this wrong, is to have such teaching defined as disturbing the peace. It would be such if it were true that God guides the ruler directly without the intervention of the members of the social system. I submit that there is a more valid model of the relationship between God and country than that which supposes blind trust in the rulers on the part of the people and an exemption from accountability for industrialists on the naive basis that the economy operates to the common good if left unmolested by the policy (Bentham). More valid, I am arguing, is a model according to which God acts through the people as they reflect on the causes of injustices in their social system. Again, I am not saying that this is new. I am saying that it does not appear in the religious education materials, as stemming from religious commitment, as regularly as does the exultant theme of God guiding the state directly without interference of the members.

Martin Marty introduces his explanation of the great awakening in America by reviewing the rise of nationalism in Germany. He says in part:

> Effective continental nationalism had to wait for the latter years of the Enlightenment and the years of romantic awakening. In Germany, for example, the philosopher Hegel gave metaphysical and religious reasons for seeing the divine plan come to a consummation in the rise of Prussia. Protestant thinkers like Johann Gottlieb Fichte and Gottfried Herder, and the theologian Friedrich Schleiermacher, were employing amazing rhetorical skills to stimulate German nationalism many decades before Prussia had risen to such prominence that it could provide armies to turn the sentiment into bloody aggression. Schleiermacher despised cosmopolitanism and considered it a vagrancy: 'Christianity demands attachment to the nation.' Whoever was not a nationalist was 'an alien in his house of God' (Quoted from Koppel S. Pinson, "Pietism as a Factor in the Rise of German Nationalism," New York, 1968).

Marty describes the rise of moral consciousness in America.

After noting, as a "sad chapter in the unfolding story," the appropriation of Protestant machinery and ideology by Nazi leadership, he says:

> Particularly instructive is the case of Protestantism's formative role in American nationalism. Here was an instance where people of many different European backgrounds, English, Scotch-Irish, Scandinavian, German, Dutch and French, could not unite on traditional grounds of common language or tradition. Yet they did have common territory and interest, and with little difficulty formed a relatively homogeneous nation in a short period of time (Marty, 1974, 258).

After providing evidence that Protestant churchmen began to invoke the most extravagant claims of American destiny, and this in millennial language related to the Second Coming of Christ, Marty concludes:

> Protestantism responds to a Scripture which in the one half of its dialectic asks men to support the 'powers that be.' The other half calls for men to obey God rather than men; to speak of God's righteousness and justice at any expense. Protestants have found it easier or more profitable to listen to the first half of its message than to the second, at the expense of the realization of a single people of God (Marty, 1974, 260).

This last comment is as true historically of Catholicism as it is of Protestantism. A current study of Catholic public pronouncements on the justice of war from 1914 through 1946 finds the Church much more concerned with the Americanization of ethnics than with the pressing issue of providing ethical guidance for a government deciding to use the people and the resources of the nation in the destruction of other people (McCarthy, 1975). On reflection it can be seen that not only did the two world wars not in fact make the world safe for democracy but they were not intended by their perpetrators to do so, as is evidenced by the fact that, as we are now aware, the same governments subsequently plotted to destroy the heads of state of certain nations—whether democratic, socialist or fascist—whose policies were not in our national interests, and to train police for the enforcement of policies that were.

Religious educators must reflect with students on how governors, that is, elected neighbors, come to perform these immoral acts in the national interest and in so doing forge a new association of religious task with patriotism. The bicentennial year provided us with an opportunity to work out at this late date what have been and what will be the intentions of teachers of religion in the future, in America and elsewhere, in view of performance in the recent past. What should be the relationship between religious education and public morals, given the effect of public decisions on the peoples of the world, and in the light of our critical review of the relationship between God and society? There are some answers. Marty ends his review of the current state of Protestantism with this summation:

> Neither the institutional nor the cultural prospects for Protestantism seem very bright to an observer in the late twentieth century. Readers of this book can see how readily Protestantism became established, authoritarian and unself-critical. Though several hundred millions remain, even the number of Protestant Church members has been in relative decline in many nations where once it was high. The Protestant era may indeed be coming or have come to its end. Perhaps the spirit of prophecy will then need new embodiments, and the witness to a transcendent God will find new incarnations as Protestantism joins other religions that, as Tillich notes, are "threatened by secularism and paganism." On the other hand, Protestantism has passed through trial and experienced decline frequently in the past and has followed such phases with renewal. It is possible that surprising forms of new life could present themselves at this century's end (Marty, 1974, 322).

Numerous writers of American intellectual history have

pointed eloquently to the bases of American society, and the very fiber of its life, in the covenant tradition of the Puritans. Our belief in human dignity, individual freedom, hope for the future and the democratic process are recognized as mandated by that covenant. However, when Marty postulates that that era of exodus may have come to an end, he may very well be correct. The civil rights movement of the 1950's and 1960's was a religious movement, a challenge to that covenanted tradition to realize its promises for a people not seeking an errand into the wilderness but space in the community, a share in the resources, in their planning, making and using. This is a tradition new to a nation that has reached its own frontiers. It calls less for skills in sending out and blessing than for skills in sharing in a non-elitist relationship of peers.

A number of commentaries on American society, including those of Michael Harrington and Robert Bellah (1975), have suggested that the future of America calls for at least the consideration of socialism as a viable form of social development. Our traditions fear that system, seeing it in the style of Germany's experiment with national socialism and Russia's state-ownership system. Out of Latin America, and in a religious context, come proposals for socialism in the framework of local participation in planning and production. We have over-used Paulo Freire's name in discussing conscientization as a way of educating geared to changing the social order, and have misused the idea of a theology of liberation (Gutiérrez, Miguez Bonino), which is really a method of theologizing in a situation in which the people are seeking their liberation from material oppression. Yet we have recognized as teachers that these methods are important enough for us to schedule new courses in this way of being religious, a way of being religious which involves not proselytizing our own religion but receiving from it the inspiration to be student as well as teacher with the poor, teacher of our skills which we choose to give away and learner of the conditions that make a change of society essential to those who are deprived. We need very much the continuation of our tradition of individual freedom and belief, our conviction that participation in decision-making is not only a right but a duty, a continuation of that firm Puritan quality that keeps us at meetings until the decisions are made and leaves us with the intention of calling our administrators to account to the assembly. This latter quality of the town meeting has been largely unused in the past several decades, although urban fair-share groups are now redeveloping these skills mandated by our Puritan heritage.

There is currently considerable fear of what is implied in Parsons' accurate description of the requisites of a society—namely, that we are in the process of developing one human society which threatens to be so controlled from the top as to be essentially inhuman even if it is primarily our society. In today's world, the economy of some nations so exceeds the boundaries of those nations that it becomes a part of their foreign policy to interfere in the government, economies, education, military training, etc., of other nations for the purpose of assuring access to the resources of those nations and the maintenance of trade relations with them designed not in the interests of the invaded nations but in the interests of the invaders. In such circumstances as these, no nation can be self-sufficient and so constitute a separate society. The claims of Western nations to self-sufficiency—their claims to constitute societies—are revealed as claims on the resources, and claims upon the social relations, of developing countries. The implications of such claims are what we are reflecting upon, I believe, as we consider American civil religion. We need religions. They are an essential reality of our lives. However, we can no longer afford, in the name of religion, to fail to call to account those who administer our commonwealth—the world commonwealth, that is—the resources of the earth's four billion people.

It is true that historically, in the tradition of the Puritan ethos, we thought of ourselves as an Exodus people in biblical terms bringing salvation to the world. We now know that, whatever we brought to the world before, what we are bringing now is not salvation. Moreover, we may now be coming to recognize as rationalizations our claims no longer to need a sacred canopy, masking the fact that we no longer desire one. We may be coming to recognize in these rationalizations a way of preparing ourselves, through private holiness and small-community solidarity, for living in a world that is managed not in terms of a functional rationality embedded in some mystical American religion, but in terms of alleged bio-chemical evolutionary processes which many of us believe are nothing more than a new ideology tailored to our new state capitalism (Wilson, 1975). The new ideology of pluralism may be expressed in such a way as to legitimate in scientific language the elimination of accountable control of a world economy which is of itself not accountable to any representative body; or alternately, it may be expressed in terms of a game-theory rationality of quid pro quo, although some of the parties to the exchange have been systematically deprived of access to their own territory (Homans, 1974; Nozick, 1975). New sociologies that minimize the necessity for participatory decision-making on the part of the poor run counter to the hope of participation which is felt in the Third World and are consistently elitist. As cases in point, we can think of the exclusion from planning of the American Indian, the American slaves and freed slaves, as well as the denial of citizenship to the black population of South Africa and Rhodesia.

The case of Rhodesia is critical since Great Britain, the nation in which our democratic heritage rests, offered an essentially non-democratic solution to the problems of that nation in the Constitutional Settlement of 1971, after negotiating in 1965 for majority rule. Our Senate and House of Representatives, staffed by our elected officials, have repeatedly voted to break the embargo initiated by the United Nations in support of the 96% black population of Rhodesia. How do we learn to use our religious moral sensitivities to honor the combined efforts of an international body deliberating with its members—that is, the United Nations—when that body has no power against us? The fact is that seventy of the rare metals we need for our durable space technology are located in Rhodesian soil and we want to be assured that, regardless of the freedoms of these people, we have secure access to the metals through the medium of whoever has title to the land. What the heads of our nation bargain for in our nation's interest with the heads of other nations—

whether or not those heads bargain in the interests of their people or ours in the interests of our people—is stable access to the resources needed for the "private" enterprise system, a system that requires and receives substantial government subsidy for its own stability even though that same government is reluctant to give the same support to our functionally unemployed population. Bargaining is done in the interests of some people, but it is demonstrably not done in the interests of the poorest two-thirds of the people of the world, nor in the interests of the twenty-three million Americans whom even Nixon's administration found to be living not in relative poverty but in real poverty, despite our trillion dollar economy. Nor do the representatives of American labor, speaking not to the interests of the poorest fifth of the American population but certainly to the segment next to them on the social pyramid, find the working people's interests to be of primary consideration in the use of our resources.

Parsons noted in his description of a society that it will be self-sufficient if the rules are affirmed by some of the people. For some time now we have operated as a society because upper- and middle-class interests were served and these were reflected in our religious and educational socialization. Now we find, as a result of recent social analysis, that even this is not so. A system in which security in retirement and medical services are purchased as commodities on the market is not in the human interest, unless some people are defined as more human than others. Our value system does not yet demand of us that services be provided for all people according to human need.

The reason for pursuing the fact that neither America nor any other nation-state any longer fits the definition of a society is to question the sacred link of religion with the nation that has been so customary down through modern history and so functional up until the economy outgrew the polity. Now we as religious people have a mission to figure out how to change our consciousness and its alliance with government as if it were sacred, to stir our imaginations and our groups to action for the purpose of bringing about a use of our resources effective for human well-being. None of our groups has innate laws of development. All groups operate in terms of some definitions commonly held by the decision-makers regarding their purpose, rights and possibilities. Thinking of our economy as having natural laws of supply and demand is simply a way of permitting the controllers to set up the alliances with other social systems which they need in order to achieve the ends they plan according to a calculus of rational self-interest. Thinking of our government as divinely-sanctioned and not in need of our surveillance permits those who win places in it to make the alliances they find to serve their interests. The failure to teach in our schools an understanding of how social systems work, or teaching that how they work is how they ought to work, given the limitations of our human natures, is just a way of extending the social ignorance that permits the persistence of coalitions and controls among those who know that these systems can be used for planned ends, and that few people will question this use since few feel that they understand the systems well enough to act effectively. Letting the media be controlled in economic interests, and failing to provide for ourselves public radio and TV time, reflect both our assumptions about the sacred character of the system and our fatalism about the inherent evil in human nature or the invincibility of the political system.

My observations may sound harsh or apocalyptic. I believe I can demonstrate that they are neither the one nor the other. Furthermore, we are in the appropriate setting for handling them. Religious education is not public education. It is not political ideology, though, in the course of history to this point, religious systems have almost invariably been co-opted by political systems shortly after their prophetic life began. There are no laws of history that determine that history repeat itself. We have had ideologies that make that claim, and they have been quite compelling, but there is a reason for that. They were posited on the assumption of human inequality and on the assumption of an innate evolution toward perfection, unfolding independently of human volition. The first of these assumptions requires that some gifted few lead the masses lest they destroy themselves through blind impulse (Freud, 1949, 1962), or else become so absorbed in the daily cycle of life that they let the important decisions go unattended (Hegel, 1953). New and popular sociological theories are pursuing this thesis further today

(Wilson, 1975). The second assumption discourages reflection on the historical process in the assurance that it will itself evolve to perfection, either because God wills it directly (Hegel) or because the natural laws of social systems will provide this directionality (Marx, Comte, early Durkheim, all Social Darwinists). This assumption has given to management planners free reign to program public and private policy in the interests of their clientele with the fair assurance that others will not use with the same skill the knowledge of how social systems work, at least until the planners have profited by some effective manipulation of the system.

In the late 1960's, Thomas Luckmann and Peter Berger presented a thesis which proved as popular as Robert Bellah's civil religion concept. Luckmann reasoned that all reality is socially constructed. Communities define their truths and work out their social organizations within these myths as the sacred limits. In much of this analysis, I think they were correct. This understanding of reality permitted the demythifying of systems of patriotism and piety. It further permitted, however, the reasoned position that pluralism was the evolutionary form for modern religious systems and that privatized religions, enabling psychic control of the individual in society and providing for the loving community, was the "best" mode of adaptation for modern social systems. Here lies the weakness of the thesis. It is argued that once the sacred canopy constituted by the shared value system was broken—historically, first with the demise of the medieval Christian empire and then with the rift in the sacred canopies (that is, the civil religions) of the individual states—then each institutional area (economy, polity, education, etc.) would be free to develop its norms according to its own functional necessities (Fenn, 1972). I submit that this is a political ideology for deflecting religious energies from public and economic concerns, leaving them to the free play of corporate industrial interests while at the same time energizing the nation's members to fill whatever work roles are available in the system. It creates a sense of powerlessness resulting from the lack of any moral consensus cutting through or standing outside of the functional requisites of the organizations in which one works. It even weakens the consciousness of a class system by fostering the idea of the normality of a mass-elite society. What I am claiming is that the very analysis, despite its critical interest, acts to legitimate a mode of exploitation that could be addressed effectively with social action.

The need for an international law system for the review and regulation of national affairs does not imply the need for building a superstate. National states can be functional within a network of governments. What is needed is that the people in each territory discover the goodness and possibility of being responsible in some transcendent fashion for their social organizations, including their national government and economy, and that they develop a facility for calling administrators to account to them for the faithful fulfillment of their mandates. This does require a spiritual identity with the peoples of the world, a growing sense of peer relations with other peoples and with their solidarity groupings, a growing set of shared moral values that touch the conscience and guide actions, new understandings of what constitutes sin and an expanded sense of responsibility for corporate sin and corporate life—tasks religious educators can effectively adopt once they shed a naive acceptance of the inevitability of the status quo.

There is a rising concern among members of many different denominational churches and within the branches of Judaism, as well as in the ethnic Catholic churches, for the application of principles of social justice to current situations where there is manifest need for them. This direction of action and reflection does not at this time have the enthusiasm of novelty about it because the movements that gave rise to it are dormant. It is now the task of religious educators to work it into the socialization of the people who are learning. The hopeful factor in this trend is that, despite the fact that there is a certain danger in the task since it is not in the interests of the economy, it is in the interest of people. The tight fit between economy, polity and religion so characteristic of the self-sufficient society violates the rights of developing peoples. What generates anxiety is that naive religious educators can be or become the instruments for generating or sustaining a new false consciousness —that is, a new legitimation of exploitative economic-political arrangements,

4
Religion and American Culture Today*

"God is the most important symbol in terms of which we come to understand our world" (Kaufman). God has been named Warrior, King, Lord, Creator, Master, Father, Son, Holy Spirit, Provider, Friend, Consoler, and Dead. The names of God have been directly related to the experience of the people who have done the naming. In those names, churches have been organized, flourished and died—different churches for different groups of people, making specific adaptation in terms of nature, self, residence community and society at large. God-talk has always been social, even where the encounter with God has taken a wide variety of forms—some very private, some communal, some societal and some purely cultural (that is, related in symbol to some earlier social context but retaining or re-creating meaning for one or more persons trying to exist in an uncongenial social or physical environment). Religion in America today embraces all these forms of the encounter with God, as well as some forms now reduced to routine ritual and containing no encounter with God at all. As an object of analysis with a view to evangelization, it is possible to make some sense out of this apparent smorgasbord of religious expression. Because our efforts to make contact with the sacred (that is, what is set apart and forbidden) and to experience the holy (that is, that which is not bound by any convention) are socially constructed, they take recognizable and definable forms.

*Paper presented at the Exploratory Consultation on the Evangelization of 80,000,000 Unchurched Americans, sponsored by the Paulists, Glenmary Missioners, Josephites, the U.S. Catholic Mission Council and Catholic University, Marriotsville Retreat House, Maryland, and Catholic University, Washington, D.C., November 12, 1975.

New Religious Groupings

For the analysis of religion within the rise of modern capitalism, sociologists have for the past several decades been satisfied with the analytic categories of church, sect, cult, denomination and mysticism (Troeltsch). Today we look with wonder at the spate of new religious expression. Since the turn of the 1970's, enthusiasm—once coded by Ronald Knox into Corinthians, Montanists, Donatists, Albigenses, Anabaptists, Quakers, Jansenists, Quietists, Convulsionaries, Moravians, Wesleyans, Irvingites, Shakers, Perfectionists, etc. (Knox, 1950)—now includes the following: the highly authoritarian and sexist Children of God; the God-making Divine Light Mission of Maharaj-ji; the doctrinaire Process Church that intertwines God and Satan in a single symbol of cross and serpent; the Hare Krishna chanters trancing themselves into visible rejection of our middle-class conventions; the Jesus Movement, so attractive to Jewish youth, speaking of Jesus' love on the streets of the kibbutz and in Jerusalem; the Moon followers preparing for the new authoritarian world state; the UFO-seekers awaiting immediate transport out of a hostile world; the college graduates sitting in yoga position delighting in altered consciousness and their beautiful bodies; the Transcendental Meditation practitioners taking time out from the office or from cab-driving to put life together in controlled emptiness; the business executives paying either to develop mind control despite the agitation of their jobs or to release their tensions in loving interpersonal encounter groups; and the charismatics providing a new mode of acceptance for harassed family members who have projected on one another the contradictions unresolved in the social order, an acceptance that establishes or re-establishes friendliness among strangers and psychic release from daily strain (at least until the new order sets in, establishing new strictures with divine sanction). And while all this experimentation with religious expression in cult and code captures the imagination and psychic energies of groups of worshipers large and small, still others, directly seeking community with or without God, experiment with tightly-knit and ordered forms of commune life (Kanter, 1972), or else take to the road in a new hoboism. The Latter Day

Saints, the Christian Scientists and now the devotees of the Meher Baba movement, like Jehovah's Witnesses, remind us that when our society turns out to be less than Christian in its structure, people can yet cope with it by withdrawing allegiance from whatever aspect of that structure has been found wanting. What can happen in time, however, is that, as in the case of the Mennonites today, what was protest in one era becomes the custom of a new era and the sect once scorned and ridiculed comes to be imaged in the law of the land and its rule of life. (Zaretsky)

The Fall of Civil Religion and the Rise of the Black Church

The many renditions of the meaning of the "turbulent sixties" given by intellectuals (Bell, 1971), historians (Ahlstrom, 1972) and victims (Frazier and Lincoln, 1963) indicate compellingly that "the American moral and religious tradition was tested in this decade and found wanting" (Ahlstrom, 1972). For Protestants and Catholics alike, church attendance peaked in 1957. This constituted the height, and was followed by the decline, of civil religion in America. The best indicator of the demise of civil religion is found in the death of the Negro church in America and the rise of the Black church after 1966. Here I refer to the insightful explanation by E. Franklin Frazier of how the menial role assigned to black slaves and freed-slaves in America, and programmed into the American division of labor, was effected through their conversion to Christianity—a process continuing down through the 1930's—and of the awareness of this menial designation growing in the course of Blacks reflecting on their experience.

The Black experience parallels in some respects that of Catholic ethnics assigned in turn to the unskilled, semi-skilled and public service roles and to life in ghettos maintained by ever so subtle discrimination until the 1940's. This ethnic church was a moral whole with a social consciousness, within which the older generation of American Catholics was educated. After

1940, it became a suburban and small-town church very much like the Protestant denominations and the Jewish synagogue communities. It was of these local churches that Will Herberg wrote (Herberg, 1960). It was their lack of spirit, and the lack of any worker church of note in Western Europe and Latin America, that stimulated Pope John XXIII to call a Council for the purpose of *aggiornamento.* By 1960, the old religious symbols were mere cultural relics and the churches moral wholes constituting local enclaves serving their own interests and closed to their immediate neighbors beyond any possibility of Christian love for the people of God. In this context, the current interest in the revival of ethnic churches in the city, and the new growth since 1970 of the conservative churches in the suburbs, signal the emergence of new islands of safety rather than the promise of liberty and justice for all; but, given the dynamics of all social history they too share the possibility of redemption through evangelization. Meanwhile, the failure of the civil rights movement to make available the American dream to American Blacks gave rise in the mid-1960's to the Black church, born along with the Black Manifesto. The outcome of this new moral consciousness is not yet clear since that dialectic is still in process. At any rate, this was the first major evidence that civil religion in America had lost its charism. These somewhat obscure references and observations now need clarification through a review of what happened after the peak year of church attendance in 1957.

In the mid-1950's, Will Herberg's *Protestant, Catholic, Jew* described in stereotypical fashion the way the church in the American suburb had developed, as did Gibson Winter's *The Suburban Captivity of the Churches* five years later. These sociological studies described the same phenomenon addressed by William H. Whyte in *The Organization Man,* namely, the growing homogenization of middle class life, the fitting of the middle class into a moral corset designed to provide for the political-economic system role-players conditioned to take their places in producing goods and services not in the interests of people but rather at the expense of the growing number of the world's poor.

This marriage of church and political economy would not be an issue for us today were not Christianity an artisans' religion—a religion, that is, of those who work with their hands—rooted in a concept of justice that emerged in biblical times through the experience of a people exiled from the source of their livelihood and seeking a promised city. But Christianity *is* an artisans' religion, of people who work with their hands as well as with their heads (Weber, 1963). Like all religions, it has constantly been co-opted by intellectuals (those who do not work with their hands) to the role of legitimating the status quo, but its affirmation of prophecy as a mode of social reform constantly calls it back to that one standard of judgment: When the rules of a society are applied, do people suffer—or do the rules embody their freedom? Religions both celebrate rules—*religare* has to do with order—and provide judgment upon the rules. Judgment upon the rules of American civil society constitutes the basis of the social movements of the 1960's, for those rules were found wanting. In biblical language, those who heard the prophet—in this case a peasant pope—left their gifts at the altar and went off to right the wrongs of the society. As that task is still in process, they have not yet returned. Those who hear the prophet are always few in number but they give the worshiping community its spirit and their absence is experienced by the community as anomie, because in the absence of those who have left the community to transform the unjust society the old rules no longer have life and the new rules do not yet exist. Small communities of Christians still worship here and there, sustaining their own life, but experimentation is no substitute for a living moral community. The teachers and preachers are searching for their materials but they as yet scarcely recognize what is the truly holy task, namely, the making of the just society.

The captivated church of the suburb, for which seminary training still prepares candidates for ministry, scarcely knows the city with its constant inflow of members from remote and rural areas. As these city people view the media, they develop rising expectations of a share in the great society portrayed in advertisement as in the elementary school reader and catechism.

Forced in many cases to come to the city as economic development took possession of their rural territory or stopped the flow
of services to their homes, they find the city dreary, neglected
and, given the pressing need for such things, sadly lacking in job
opportunities, medical care, free schools and services for the elderly. A system exists for providing these services but the spirit
for doing so with loving concern is lacking. The system is dis-
criminatory and lacks soul. There are too many people, too nar-
row a tax base and too unstable a job market to sustain or develop the services which the advertisements promise. But the
people in the suburbs hardly know this. And the religion which
has sustained the suburb is inadequate for the life of the city.

The old religious model of helping the poor, of alleviating
the results of poverty, is not adequate to the numbers now in
need of human services. It broke down as a charity system
because the system of production and allocation of goods to
which it was attached proved incapable of delivering goods and
services commensurate with the real human need. It emerged as
neither holy nor evangelical. It had become secular. What this
means historically is that the production of goods and services,
their design and use, is not in the people's interest but is a function of profit-making. This is reflected in the supplying of
health, education and welfare to certain people and not to
others. The system of production and distribution lacks imagi-
native planning because it is unrelated to the holy.

The hearts of Americans are not stirred—in church, in
school or in the mass media—to celebrate a service system that
provides health-care for the sick, schools for the illiterate and
security for the superannuated and chronically ill. In the church
of the suburb the services are adapted to the organizational job
market, open only to a few and servicing the interests of fewer.
That church sustains only that life, the lives of only those people. As Michael Harrington well demonstrated in *The Other
America*, the poor were hidden by the new highway system and
thus became as remote to the consciousness of suburban America as the people in rural Rhodesia, the South African reserves
and the roadless wastes of northeast Brazil. In the early fifties—
with McCarthyism strongly representing as subversive those

who called attention to the inequities of the commonwealth—
our universities, churches and media were lulled, for fear of
being labeled disloyal, into mere middle-class consciousness and
into believing in and celebrating an island of safety, namely,
suburban America. Here the churches of the Herberg thesis
flourished—Protestant, Catholic and Jewish. Eisenhower could
declare, "Our government makes no sense unless it is founded
in a deeply felt religious faith—and I don't care what it is,"
because—as Machiavelli's prince would understand—a religious
people is a docile people, and a docile people is essential to the
development of an economy which is not people-oriented.

However, just as a century ago the workers of Europe
became disenchanted with the churches because church personnel exhibited a naiveté about or resistance to addressing their
poverty, so today the welfare recipients and the only temporari-
ly employed segments of the American economy, chafing under
the inequities of urban life, ignore the urban churches. These
churches, geared as they are to serving a declining ethnic clientele, are now emptying. Meanwhile, the poor are now listening
more intently to those prophetic voices that are speaking to the
truth of their immediate experience, that is, to the fact that
what the media proclaim as the good life in America does not
provide for them; that in fact the green-grass life of the duplex
and automobile is closed to them by zoning laws, by restrictive
covenant, by realtor collusion; that red-lining in their neighborhoods, experimentation and inadequate staffing in their hos-
pitals and political neglect in their schools (situated as they are
on land already designated for purposes other than those of the
poor), make neighborhood development almost impossible. In a
country with a booming trillion-dollar economy planning for a
single-product system—namely, armaments for export—the
poor are as expendable as the citizens of any foreign population
of non-workers whether they be in Korea (as was the case in the
1950's) or southeast Asia, northern Ireland, northern Africa,
Chile, Brazil, Bangladesh, Ethiopia or Angola today. Since
Christianity is an artisans' religion, it is clear that the groups I
have dwelt on are those from whom Christianity has been wrested in the interest of maintaining islands of safety in the suburbs.

The Bible, Social Justice and Moral Community

The good news in the 1950's was still in the book. It only needed a minister to preach it, and a community to respond. Martin Luther King, chosen by the confluence of circumstances that marks any vocation, symbolizes that minister. And, given the new ministry, the church-as-movement began its trek throughout the land. Civil rights for blacks represented a real religious call in a country that had at its inception forged a covenant between an angry God and a non-conforming people, people who had felt the human exploitation of workers in a newly-industrialized England, a country of yeofolk, once the merchant elite co-opted England's episcopal chairs. Civil rights for black people in the U.S., where the Statue of Liberty is marked with an invitation to all the weary of the world to come and be free, was a religious call to American Catholics in a special way. Catholicism had a tradition of missions and retreats, where those who had personally sinned by pride, covetousness, lust, anger, gluttony, envy and sloth could come apart and rest a while, commune with God and neighbor, approach the stranger as friend, bond again in repentance for personal sin and go home feeling that the Spirit was indeed moving all over the land. Catholics are called, in other words, to welcome the stranger into the community of the faithful as into an ever-widening circle, a community without walls.

From Jonathan Edwards, to Emerson and Thoreau, to Billy Sunday and Billy Graham, Americans had a tradition of purging souls of entrepreneurial guilt by singing, repenting and hoping for heaven. This old tradition, however, was not so much directed to opening communities to strangers in need as it was to stirring the oppressed to communal solidarity sufficient to energize their striking out into the wilderness to found a new society in the image of the one from which they were excluded. America's civil religion *was* an Exodus tradition and its spirituality focused on building the walled community for the saints, defined as the members. On the other hand, the civil rights movement focused on a different human need, one the Spanish were more skilled in meeting, which would involve allowing for an invasion of the closed community with new life—because the resources had expanded and there was more capacity to share. America's civil religion had no old tradition for coping with the invasion of one community by another. It knew only how to cope with one stranger at a time, and then by having the stranger assimilate to the dominant ethos.

The Unchurched Catholic Doctrine

Across denominations, a few church people clearly saw this different human need expressed in the demands of the 1960's. The frontier was now closed. The demand of the civil rights movement for justice under the law was a call for a new opening of communities for the residence of those excluded. The Gospel basis for this new demand revealed the fact that the law to deal with this demand did not yet exist, because the law in existence was geared to the protection of property and these new invaders had come to America as themselves property. The evil right to use people as property was contained in the law and in the economic theory, but the right of all to their use of property was yet to be fashioned. This was a new religious call—a call to review the law in the light of the Gospel, to reveal its limitations and to legislate not for the protection of property but for the protection of people.

This new focus was clearest to those who were moved by the new religious call, that is, to enlarge the community of those reckoned as equals. The extent of human neglect under the law became more and more visible to them. Moreover, this new consciousness moved quickly to include not only civil rights for the black community (on the move from rural to urban America as a function of the changed uses of technology), but also the rights of students to participate in decisions about education on the American campus (once it was discovered that their textbooks were geared to class advantage and not to liberal education and that faculty were blinded to their own consumer education), the rights of nations subjected to the evil of basing a world economy on the production and distribution of lethal weapons intended for the slaughter of human beings, and the human rights of Third World peoples coming to consciousness all over the world that the land on which they resided and the use of that land was theirs to determine, in their own interests and for their own development, as peers in a community of nations —and not the prerogative of very powerful and over-demanding corporations, controlling states representing the interests of less than one-third of the world's four billion people.

The new religious concern for people's development, over a hundred years in the making and referred to—disparagingly by some—as the "social gospel," was affirmed by the Catholic Church through a succession of Gospel-based documents marked by growing sensitivity to social issues—beginning with *Rerum Novarum* and developing through *Quadragesimo Anno, Mother and Teacher, Peace on Earth, The Dogmatic Constitution on the Church, On the Development of Peoples, A Call to Action,* and recently in the Synodal Document *Justice in the World.* These successive stances gradually located the Catholic charism at the side of the poor of the world as an ally helping them to claim what belongs to them by right. Analyzed, these documents indicate a radical change in formal Catholic policy, from an old focus on the alleviation of the results of poverty to a new focus on the elimination of its causes. This new focus supports the presence of the poor at the planning table, at the world health conferences, and at the Assemblies for the New Economic Policy of the United Nations. Nor should the significance be overlooked of the recent celebration by the developing nations of the tenth anniversary of Pope Paul's visit to the United Nations. The transition reflected an exciting Gospel-based message in the tradition of the jubilee and the sabbatical rules of Leviticus 25. To the complacent suburb, however, it was a disturbance of the peace.

For those seeking the ease that accompanies the leisured life, all this activity focusing on the rights of the poor was annoying, even if the poor do constitute two-thirds of the world; even if we do have a technology that could but does not get used to address their needs; even if the Gospel is defined as bringing them good news. Accordingly, the new focus was met with con-

fusion if not indifference. To the demands of the poor in the
city, in rural areas and in the third world, those addressed at
home and on the beach responded with yawns, with chagrin or
with continued "Cabaret." Except for the marginal clergy who
were denigrated for their stands, church persons resisted these
stirrings oriented toward the affirmation of new life-space for
the poor. Theological innovators were censured for stirring up
the campus because the symbols of their new behavior seemed
grotesque amid the Greek and baroque symbols of the schools,
their tone too strident, their emotional life too fragile, their association with the poor too uncomfortable. The schools of ministry scarcely stocked the new documents; still less did they
revamp their courses to teach them or train people to preach
this socially oriented good news. In many places the teaching of
systematic Western European theology went on as if the failure
of existing structures to provide for two-thirds of the world's
people had not destroyed the credibility of the theologies that
affirmed these structures. Seminary student applications declined, seminarians became more characterized by timidity than
by youthful vision, and church people wondered what had happened to the Spirit.

The Unchurched Student

Into cities teeming with social problems, problems of
neighborhoods closed-in-siege against the encroachment of one
race or another, came Blacks as Muslims and Black church people developing as tall men and beautiful women who could hold
their heads high and make demands on a reluctant and frightened local political system, corrupted by a century of working-
class patronage instead of bank-sponsored local investment and
development. Into these same cities came American middle-
class youth from the private, state and community colleges,
youth whose parents had for the most part not gone to college,
full of expectation that the American dream would now be
theirs by reason of their higher education. They came to the
cities, fired by descriptions of America's urban problems. They

came from the social science and literature classes to do their field work in the city, where they learned with heightened indignation of the disparities of the American system they had been taught to love. They saw the city. For many it was the inequity of their own working-class town situation that they were discovering, but even for youth who were neither black nor chicano —almost all of them—the shock of the manifest neglect in the decaying American poverty zones of city and rural areas was overwhelming. With new zeal, this five percent of the student body attempted to do something about what they had discovered. However, unilateral planning, limited consultation, temporary interest, naive economic models, strong political resistance to their efforts and exposure to neglect made this onslaught of youthful enthusiasm and earnest effort a painful and difficult experience. The response of city personnel was one of hostile, frightened, angry, indignant resistance. The experience of thwarted youth is not a pleasant one for precariously-structured urban systems, themselves occupying only a fragile place in a national and world economy. Four years of angry encounter analyzed in mimeographed handouts, long evening meetings and newly-recognized action groups fired by genuine concern for injustice in the urban situation, shaped the youthful vocation to action.

Some sought moral and spiritual guidance from the churches. The problems of these youthful volunteers, however, were scarcely understood by church people trained in the tradition of systematic theology, ensconced in the suburban parish and empty urban church, patterned by life in the pastor's house where the curate boarded, or by life next door in the over-routinized convent. The church people spoke from another world, where they endured the present through heightened routine while waiting for the Second Coming. The students brought up in a regular urban or suburban parish recognized this unawareness and questioned the relevance of such a style of religious living in a city, country and world characterized by problems of human need of the dimensions now exposed to them. For a while they expected that the same new vision that they experienced would have touched the priests and sisters whose aid they solicited, but they soon learned to turn to their own resources, to the detached clergyman and sister who, rejected by their communities as by their confused and bewildered families, moved outside the system in order to serve.

A new island of safety developed among these wounded workers, a new disenchantment, a new community of those losing faith in the charism of the institutional church. It seemed as if the old prayers and retreats were talking about these very things to which they now felt called with a persuasion they were certain went beyond personal preference, but the tired and routinized parish stood intransigent, clothed with the solemnity of the centuries but bogged down in idle contradiction of a problem that needed their resources and enthusiasm. The old symbols lost their charism. How marvelously apt were those old brick buildings and those big frame houses for the people of the city to gather in to reflect together about remaking the city. But they were not open to them, and the only language spoken within them was foreign to these new living problems. Youth turned elsewhere for their temporary needs. But the people of the city became even more isolated, because a church called to action either responds or dies.

The Unchurching of the Working-Class Parish

The hearts of many were in panic. The families of youth were upset when their liberal sons and daughters returned from college with new insights and demands, and they wondered why their dream of upward mobility through expanded job opportunities open to college graduates, far from being the reward of their college-educated children, was generating a new and more alienating unrest than the frustration of the menial tasks of the earlier immigrant years. What had they done wrong? Some youth, overwhelmed by the alienation from family and friends and needing as they now did an even tighter moral corset, repressed the guilt of their urban failure and fitted even better into the old church structure, becoming part of the process of the growth of the conservative churches. But now the routine which before had reinforced a stable life of simple goodness repressed a hidden guilt. Anomie set in. Following the old rules just did not elicit the same reinforcement anymore. Church membership for them declined through unexplainable malaise. They had not time now for the apparently meaningless ceremony. The old symbols, not yet put to the test of experience, lacked life, for they were not yet identified with response to the prophetic call to stand with the poor.

In this context, consciousness-altering experiences of a wide variety of forms provided respite. For some they are an escape from a painfully inadequate social situation; for others they are a temporary haven for revitalizing psychic energy and world perspective; for still others they are a way of life as good as any for moving beyond the institutional. For Catholic Christians they are religiously neutral to the degree that the call of the poor is ignored, denied or set aside. "Altered states of consciousness" may provide space and experience for the generation of a genuinely new consciousness, but they do not themselves constitute it.

The new social consciousness in world perspective is catholic by definition. What Catholicism provides as Catholicism, and not as the rationalization it and other religions often become (Dawson, 1948), is a definition of community that includes all the people, the fostering of an ethic that affirms life, the sponsoring of programs that provide for the development of peoples, the celebration of the Eucharist that is transforming for everybody, and a community without walls marked by a Christian love for the poor.

The New Uses of Religious Techniques

The people who bore the heat of the movements for civil rights for Blacks, for participation in decision-making by youth and other minorities, and for the elimination of death for small nations by lethal weaponry have experimented with yoga, transcendental meditation, retreats and other forms of private religion. Some joined the community-making experiments, some continued their pursuit of new ideologies, some returned to the pews, and some became totally alienated. All have available on reflection experience beyond their own old interests. They are potential candidates for evangelization.

There are pitfalls, however, so much of the enthusiasm and malaise having already been packaged for sale. The techniques for reaching out beyond the institutional were gathered up and marketed for the weary professional hassled by demand and disappointment, so that the business executive whose conscience, so pricked by these problems of injustice that his enthusiasm for the unreflected use of mass persuasion was dimmed, could get his mind and emotions under control and continue on in his unreflected way. This use of spiritual technique, refined in the medieval East as Zen for the Samurai class and newly affirmed in the West for its effectiveness in quieting the mind and opening the heart to new life, is now a commodity on the consumer market. Any religious inspiration could be diverted to the same end.

Families harassed by the demands of social justice from their committed youths, youths themselves confused and hurt by their families, community people who had chosen human services as their life work for a whole range of unreflected reasons, and church people saddened by their empty pews have found communality in the enthusiasm of the charismatic movement because of its focus on kindness. Its new life is fostered by rhythmic music and moves toward a heightened experience of community and the purging of those angry feelings toward the immediately-present other. The God-language, so familiar in content, is now publicly expressed; once whispered, it is now shouted. For those long absent from the churches, there is space here for renewed and healing religious expression in the context of a new companionship. These experiences, together with those available in the communes and conservative churches, all provide for a restoration of life. Without address to the evils of social class, however, they can do little more than create new bonds of security against the very problems the Gospel intended to resolve.

Conclusion

One cannot expect to understand the present religious scene in America if one does not juxtapose to all the frenetic activity and experimentation with religious forms the larger reflection on religion and society that stems from the critiques of Hegel, Marx, Durkheim, Weber, Malinowski and others. Talcott Parsons, Robert Bellah, Andrew Greeley and the current sociologists of religion describe and analyze the practice of religious forms in a society with a given political, economic and social class structure, a structure having its creed, code and cult harmonized in some kind of articulation and tension with the daily and annual cycle of life. They explain the current functions and dysfunctions of religion. Their explanations of the death-of-God focus of theology in the 1960's is instructive. Finding names for God has been the theological task down through the centuries. We who speak to God use our own words. Whether we label God "God" (itself a Western cultural factor), Warrior, King, Lord, Master or Father, we are talking in a language rooted in our cultural experience (Daly, 1973), all of which experiences are part of the social systems that have, as we now know, exploited some people as slaves, serfs or expendable units if they did not adapt themselves to the work load assigned by the dominating decision-makers. Hegel has argued that the principle of reason informs the whole historical process and, though human efforts to organize societies with world views have fallen short of perfection, still for its times each was imbued with the Spirit. Marx argued that the charismatic moment was just that—a moment—and that soon men in interaction with one another laid burdens on the powerless that they were unwilling to bear themselves. He argued further that men called this division of labor holy, celebrating it in religions, laws, philosophies and arts that are merely epiphenomenal to the social-class system they wanted to develop, that those who had power over the lives of others through control of education and the media would teach—with the force of militia and fining and incarceration behind them—the goodness of the existing division of labor.

Most Americans think of religion today as civil religion, a

non-denominational-type religion that is really not practiced by anyone but which in some mystical way legitimates the American way of life. Christianity, practiced by a few people and named by many as their traditional affiliation, is not such a religion. Catholic evangelists have to return to the Gospel and to the study of their tradition to see what evangelization calls for today. Out of the life of the church in the world, the task of evangelization has been defined as bringing the good news to the poor. The poor have heard that news and are rising up to demand what is theirs in justice—health services when they are ill, education when they are illiterate, security of shelter and clothing and food when they are old, maimed or too young to work, and jobs when they are adults. The times reveal that little of what we have tried in the past constitutes good news to the poor today. But a new spirit is moving over the land and it has its life where people gather to pray and worship as well as where they work and suffer. It calls for a whole new theological outlook, the elements of which are already part of the dialogue and action of people who feel comfortable in reaching out across traditional barriers (Gutiérrez, 1973). It calls for a commitment to social change that may require a greatly reduced enthusiasm for the celebration of states as societies, and a greatly increased enthusiasm for the development of peoples. It denies that social class is of the nature of things. It is probably the case that God is and will be dwelling now and in the near future where people suffer dire poverty, and is acting with them to eliminate these conditions; and that those who are out on the mountain seeking God beyond the rim of human experience may miss the reality, the pillar of light in the dust of the city, the reality signaled in the blackness of the church and in the gender of the language about God.

We are directed by Matthew 5:23-24 to leave our gifts at the altar when a brother or sister has something against us, to go out and right the wrong and then to return for the worship service. Whole groups of sisters and brothers are telling us at this time that we are needed where the inequities exist, needed to affirm the rights of people to share in the goods and services of the world, and especially to share in planning how these will be developed in the interest of their survival. An artisan people relies on the priest to lead the assembly in prayer and worship, in language that makes sense to them; with a message and a meaning that draws on their altruism and their allegiance to the good of the community, against the pull of selfish longings, with the assurance that their happiness rests in their response to this call and that their efforts will be affirmed by the community. The poor have to rely on the magic, that is, the hope beyond reason that the transformation of their lives will happen now. The rich need to understand what it all means in a language they understand. The church, then, carries the mandate to provide the magic, to train the priests and to affirm the theology that assures that the Gospel is catholic—that is, for the people. In this age, that assurance has been defined as liberty and justice for all. The problem is that as yet it is not a magic that works for the poor, not a gospel that is preached by the priests, and that the theology to realize it has hardly been shaped and is not as yet formally taught in the seminary or novitiate. Until this task is in process no evangelization will be effective, beyond a rationalization for class interests which is presently disenchanting the people.

I would venture to propose that Paulo Freire has provided in conscientization a form for the new pedagogy. Gutiérrez has provided in the theology of liberation the beginning of one dimension of the dialectic for the new theology—the other being a theology of relinquishment for the advantaged. Women will supply the language about God, the Black church a model for the celebrating community, Catholicism the assembly to be gathered. All the current religious experimentation will provide styles congenial to different peoples, local churches the places for the herald to come, Amilcar Cabral the model of the just person, religious orders of women the years' experience with experimentation, the Bible the good news to be interpreted, and the poor the place to begin—because where they are is where God dwells.

5
Reconciliation*

The Christian stance toward societal structures has radically changed because of Vatican II and Pope John XXIII's *Peace on Earth*. The Church is once again standing with the poor. The rich man has to contemplate the camel and the needle as the real dilemma once more, rather than produce smaller camels and bigger needles. This means to me that there is just no way now for claiming that the rich, white, male and older people are on an equal footing of demand with the poor, black, female and younger people in the sense that their interests receive the same kind of priority from the perspective of the Christian commitment. The new emphasis on commitment to justice and peace puts the process of reconciliation between groups into an action focus, calling for conscientization (Freire, 1970, 19).

Karl Marx has well said:

Men make their own history, but they do not make it just as they please: they do not make it under circumstances chosen by themselves, but under circumstances directly encountered, given and transmitted from the past. The tradition of all dead generations weighs like a nightmare on the brain of the living (Marx, 1959, 97).

For centuries the rich man has determined the destiny of peoples. Today, two-thirds of the people of the world live below subsistence when we have a technology that could but does not get used to provide basic goods and services for all the people. The Third World—that is, those unaligned poor people who are

*A talk delivered at the Symposium on Reconciliation and Ritual at the University of San Francisco, January 4, 1975.

becoming aware of their rights to the goods of the world—are reaching out with a new sense of their own worth and dignity and demanding their share of the earth's wealth. The rich are being asked to return the land to the people as Leviticus directed for the jubilee, each fiftieth year. Had that directive been followed down all these centuries, the land would have been left in the hands of the people, or at least it would have been provided by law that the land be systematically returned after each era of greed and exploitation had wrested it from the less powerful and unfortunate.

The process of conscientization, so named by Paulo Freire, is an educative function of teaching poor peasants of northeast Brazil how to claim their rights under the law and to learn to be literate as they become aware of the political, economic and social oppression of their society and take action to right discovered wrongs. It is an action-reflection process, a praxis in the educational tradition. It is also a way to reconciliation, if the people becoming aware of their own rights and implementing them are met by other people involved in the corresponding process of letting go the power and wealth they unjustly hold.

The Problem

Is reconciliation between these groups—rich and poor, black and white, older and younger, men and women—in the best interests of all the parties concerned? If we are seeking reconciliation, then there must have been a previous conflict and separation. What were the causes of the rift? What did "they" want that "we" had? Did the rich happen to be white, older and men, the poor happen to be black, younger and women? If this is the case, then the task is clear. Reconciliation will follow when the white older men share their wealth with the poor, the blacks, the young and women. Wealth provides for the goods and services needed for human living. It belongs to the people. Why some have so much of it and others so little is a biblical problem of sin, avarice, pride, ambition, etc. But it is not mere wealth that is involved in the rift between these dichotomous groupings. The rich, white, older men have something else that the poor, black, younger people and women need. And that is power. Those deprived of power have been telling us this for some time now. The revolutions of the past hundred years represent the poor telling us their need for more adequate sources of power. The civil rights movement of the 1950's and the Black power movement of the 1960's were the voice of Black America. At the same time, the students have spoken in the free speech movement originating at Berkeley, and the women for the past century have been speaking of the need for liberation. Power, the capacity to get other people to do what you want, the opportunity to be taken seriously by others beyond their selective altruism, is essential for human development. The right to participate in the decisions that affect one's life constitutes real power, participation on one's own terms.

Demanding power followed an awareness that when people make decisions for other people they make them against the expressed interests of those people. The oppressed found out that the decisions made for them, even by their "benefactors," were made in the interests of the giver. Whether what was given was financial aid to underdeveloped nations through the World Bank and AID program, or Southern Africa's medical program for African workers enabling them to work harder, or the Office of Economic Opportunity's programs for the poor in the city, or the national, state and local welfare programs funded by the American tax system, or the military aid to Vietnam, or the public educational system and its auxiliary, the parochial educational system, or even the Christianity the colonial governments sponsored for the natives—in all cases, where participatory decision-making has been lacking, the outcome of decisions has been in the interest of those making the decisions. Whether they be local residential community leaders or corporation managers or private college faculty senates or diocesan chancery officers, the fact is that no people can speak another's truth. This does not mean that planning programs should not exist. Far from it. It does mean, however, that the management of programs, no matter what they are, will provide for the interests only of those whom the specific managers represent, those to whom they see themselves accountable. Any group whose destiny is involved in a plan and which is not represented by its self-chosen representatives whom it can call to account is certain to be acted against in the planning, whether wittingly or unwittingly.

This is what the poor, the blacks, the young and the women have tried to communicate in the past fitful decade. It has proved true, however, that no group, no matter how loud its protest, will be taken seriously by those doing the planning unless they have sufficient potential to disrupt the outcome to warrant their being included in the plans. If the planners perceive, however, that by giving a share of the planning to one articulate segment of the dispossessed others will later come forward with similar demands, then they will organize with other power groups to resist the "intrusion." Should this happen, then the expectant oppressed can seek allies among other oppressed, now recognized as peers with a common interest. The power struggle is then joined. The reason this happens is that what bothers the targets of protest is not the demands and their justification but the hostility. The concern of the secure is that their lives are being disrupted, their interests jeopardized. They want to get the horsefly off their hides and return to normal. But the normality longed for by the rich, white, older men has been the same control and distribution system which they have traditionally managed through political, economic, scientific, cultural, psychic and religious formulae.

The solution of the resulting conflicts is relatively simple to state. It does not lie in the altruistic magnanimity of the morally moved rich, white, older men giving of their largesse, but rather in the recognition that the structures of social systems that allow for the continual return of the proffered "gifts" to the original holders and their posterity are organized in their interests to fulfill this intended end, despite any appearances to the contrary. It is the function of the social scientist to determine how this happens so consistently down through the ages despite protests both spontaneous and organized.

Assumptions about Human Nature

Social scientists have suggested some interesting if invalid explanations for the process. The most popular one is that of natural hierarchy. It has several different garbs depending on whether one approaches the question philosophically, theologically, natural-scientifically or historically. The different versions go like this: (a) Ontologically speaking, the natural order of society is given in its historical patterns. The reason that certain persons, groups, colors or sexes are dominant is that the natural hierarchy of human worth is expressing itself through the genes, the culture, the times. It is natural for wealth and power to rest with the naturally gifted. The task is to see that they lead altruistically. The principle is *noblesse oblige*. (b) In theological terms, God the Creator is the dominant principle, to whom we naturally refer in the generic masculine. Since we are created in God's image, then the more dominant is the more Godlike. God blesses with abundance those who do His will—and the will of God is the good of man. God did not come upon earth as a Black or a woman, so neither can they be first in His image. He did come poor and young—but He grew older. So the young can wait, and the poor—well, there are many kinds of poverty that even the rich suffer, and besides, "The poor you will always have with you." So we who are more made in God's image— white males—will decide for God concerning the riches we already have and the power we already possess. (c) The natural scientists answer the problem in their own way. The gene pool is distributed in systematic ways. No matter how you sort the people, they will interact to reproduce the natural hierarchy. Call it a meritocracy if you like, but what it means is that those in power and with the easy access to wealth will reacquire it, no matter how it gets redistributed, because the "others" will spend it carelessly, will cheat, exploit and so need to be rescued or even to pay the elite who are more professionally competent to help them out of their new difficulties. No matter the method, the possessions and the power will return to them, because, in the last analysis, the abilities are in the genes and the IQ test reveals them. So the best thing to do is to train the elite to serve the masses. (d) Historically, the argument runs this way. Look at history, any history, and you will see this same pattern of elites. There is nothing new under the sun. It all comes back, an eternal cycle.

Through all of these "social science" explanations runs the same naive set of assumptions, namely, that there is a natural distribution of rewards and that those who now have them got them because they deserved them by nature, grace and gift. In these explanations, the assumptions remain untested and do not provide for change, except in the manner of the eternal return. They encourage the learner to opt for adjustment and adaptation but not for modification or change of the manifestly unjust. They idealize the prayer of quiet, the dignity of stillness, stoicism, and the relief afforded by eternal salvation. The elite must hold firm and not be moved by the emotionalism of the desperate.

There is another kind of "social science" explanation of the legitimacy of the present distribution of goods, services and power that is called Social Darwinism. It too has its own philosophers, theologians, ethicists, scientists and historians. In this explanation, there is a magnanimity built in, if you wait long enough. It extends Darwin's theory of evolution to the social order. Here the social scientist explains that all groups of today's deprived masses, the ethnic poor, the young, the Black and the women, will one day have the experience of ascendancy that the powerful of the earth have today. It is just a matter of development. It takes time. When each group is ready, it will come into its own. There is a set of laws of history that is constantly operating to move each group closer to its full human development. The Aryans are the farthest ahead. The tall, blond, blue-eyed, broad-shouldered, athletic-looking types are the most developed, then the Mediterranean peoples, the orientals and the Blacks. According to this theory, it makes a lot of difference whom you marry and where you allocate welfare monies in seeing that the fittest survive. In fact, it is better not to have welfare programs at all. It is better to give the resources to those who are ahead in development so that the least fit will die off, leaving space on the earth for good genetic types to develop— *Lebensraum.* Hitler's *Mein Kampf* spells out the thesis in its classic form. His regime best communicates what happens to the "lesser" races that occupy desired space. Six million Jews were killed because they did not fit the body types even though intellectually and culturally they had made major contributions to the society. Religious teaching helped to affirm their inadequacy. Their deaths in gas chambers which were operated by ordinary people like you and me earning their daily bread at government-paid jobs teach us how completely a theory like this can occupy the minds of the members of a state and guide their behavior despite, or rather because of, their native education. Where could a Jewish child go to school to learn that this theory was a political act? Or, as a parallel example, how could an Algerian study medicine during the period of the French colonial control without being taught in his own native land that his cortex was differently developed from that of his French rulers and that hence he could not be expected to react with the same coolness nor reach the same stages of development. His teachers believed this theory, a theory supporting their interests, and taught it in the universities which they staffed. The Algerian who trained there, unless already conscientized, was conditioned to be the petty bureaucrat in his own land by the very information he imbibed. This, then, justified the psychotherapists', magistrates' and employers' treating the Algerian as an overgrown emotional child, whose responses were more aggressive and expressive than instrumental, because of his nature, his genes, etc. Not until the revolution called the Algerians to a hope of control over their destiny was that aggressive and expressive energy seen to be parallel to that of his French counterparts and used in reconciliation with his brothers toward the realization of their own freedom (Fanon, 1963, 249-310).

Boumédienne, president of a free Algeria, led seventy-five nations of the world in the initiation of a new economic charter for the United Nations, a charter that assures each people control over its resources and participation in all decisions concerning it. What have the powerful nations done to this proposal? Why are we reluctant to share enthusiastically in its proclamation? It is a great breakthrough in the international development of peoples. Do we not have a lurking suspicion that these "children" nations are not yet ready for this responsibility? And do we not justify this by assuring ourselves that when they are ready we will be there to help them take their rightful place? But suppose, despite our lurking suspicion, the time is now right for them to take that place, since it is now that they are willing and feel ready to do so—does not our suspicion, under these circumstances, act to prevent them from rising to this new power position? And are we not then the stumbling block to their full freedom? And who has provided us with the information that sustains the suspicion, and who withholds the information that would dissolve it? Was our hesitancy to affirm this new charter more accurately a lurking anxiety that we may have to take more of the people seriously into decision-making regarding the production and distribution of goods and services like oil and rare metals needed for advanced technology? At some point we realize that we fear other peoples' getting more power, even though we can recognize the truth of the principle that people should participate in the decisions that affect their lives. Do not the theories of natural hierarchy and of Social Darwinism make it easier for us to justify our own aspirations to elitism so that we constantly seek evidence that maybe those theories are truer than we thought? (For the most recent evidence-gathering of this kind, see Edward O. Wilson's *Sociobiology*.)

Consider these words of one of the nation's leaders—a trusted leader and yet one unaware of the real problem on account of his erroneous conception of human nature—and reflect on their implications for an understanding of the reconciliation of groups. They are the words of Abraham Lincoln on reconciliation between North and South in the 1860's:

> My paramount object in this struggle is to save the Union, and is not either to save or to destroy slavery. If I could save the Union without freeing any slave, I would do it; and if I could save it by freeing some and leaving others alone, I would also do that ("Reply to Horace Greeley," quoted in Cone, 1969, 10).

Once more, Lincoln speaks:

> I will say then that I am not, nor ever have been in favor of bringing about in any way the social and political equality of the black and white races—that I am not nor ever have

been in favor of making voters or jurors of Negroes, nor of qualifying them to hold office, nor to intermarry with white people. And I will say in addition to this that there is a physical difference between the white and black races which I believe will forbid the two races living together on terms of social and political equality. And inasmuch as they cannot so live, while they do remain together, there must be the position of superior and inferior, and I as much as any other man am in favor of having the superior position assigned to the white race (see Silberman, *Crisis in Black and White*, pp. 92-93, quoted in Cone, 1969, 10).

These sadly honest lines tell us that Lincoln freed the slaves not because of a belief but because of a demand. Had there been no demand, there would have been no freedom. Slavery and its elimination was for him at that time merely the cause of the conflict. His concern was not with the fact that people without a grasp on wealth and power were oppressed by other people. He did not yet experience the belief that people different from himself were just as human as he. He was only concerned about the resolution of conflict, the alleviation of the results of separation. He had not yet even considered the elimination of the causes.

Demands of newly-aware groups of oppressed people cannot afford to be lost in reconciliation until the oppressors recognize that the demands are justified and must be addressed before reconciliation can happen. People will die so that others may have the freedom they long for and cannot have. The powerful can organize easily in causes that public relations firms can present as good and just to those who already have status and freedom.

Once we affirm for all people the right to share in the goods of the world and the services they need to survive, then we can plan modes of reconciliation which include services for all the people, free services, beginning with those in greatest need. Income taxes arranged according to ability to pay and the intentional reduction of the distance between very high incomes and all others are far more natural places for effective social control than forcing poor people to change schools without providing better education in those schools. It is also more natural than pretending we are solving an educational problem after we have stirred up racial hatreds to prevent the program from working so that the resources can be allocated to the companies that resolve conflict instead of to the people learning to live together and using their own resources.

The anomalies that emerge from our present system of service are evident in the following account. Here is a poor man telling the rich how expensive it is to be poor. He is speaking about being poor in South Africa:

> Thus in South Africa now it is very expensive to be poor. It is the poor people who stay farthest from town and therefore have to spend more money on transport to come and work for white people; it is the poor people who use uneconomic and inconvenient fuels like paraffin and coal because of the refusal of the white man to install electricity in black areas; it is the poor people who are governed by many ill-defined restrictive laws and therefore have to spend money on fines for 'technical' offences; it is the poor people who have no hospitals and are therefore exposed to exorbitant charges by private doctors; it is the poor people who use untarred roads, have to walk long distances, and therefore experience the greatest wear and tear on commodities like shoes; it is the poor people who have to pay for their children's school books while whites get them free. It does not need to be said that it is the black people who are poor (Steve Biko, in Moore, 1974, 46).

A word of explanation. There are no poor whites in South Africa because only white people are allowed by law to do the clerical staff work and professional work, so there are more jobs than there are white people to fill them. This, of course, also makes the system inefficient, because even the inadequately educated and personally undisciplined whites receive these jobs. Needless to say, the quality of the work suffers. That the poor pay more is equally true of American society (Caplowitz, 1967). Add to this that poor people are sold illth instead of wealth

(Walter, 1973). Can we then ask for reconciliation before addressing ourselves to these injustices? Is not this address the first step in reconciliation?

Providing fewer opportunities for the poor reveals the assumptions of second-class citizenship, the assumption of either natural hierarchy or Social Darwinism. Social Darwinism pervaded race relations textbooks and welfare manuals from the time of William Graham Sumner's *Folkways,* the logic of which legitimated the Plessey vs. Ferguson case in 1896, up through our economic development programs of the 1950-1960 period. All we have to do is to compare the Marshall Plan grants given for the redevelopment of Europe with the A.I.D. loans in order to understand the process (Magdoff, 1969). My reason for pointing to these materials is not to rehash the known evils of our aid programs to underdeveloped nations but to allow us to consider here what theory of human nature undergirds our current attempts to reconcile groups that are hostile to each other. Are we intending to reconcile before the causes of the hostility on the side of the oppressed group have been eliminated? Are we secretly trying to corral the energy back into the unjust system, or to deny the injustices of the system despite the angry insistence on the part of the newly-conscious minorities that their rights and interests are not provided for in the laws and customs of the society? Or is the reconciliation really intended to affirm a new partnership in achieving those rights, changing those laws, constructing a political-economic system that does not build-in a plan for eternal return or progressive waiting until this generation of affluent and powerful die off and so escape the revolution? And, if it is the latter we intend, how do we assure ourselves or those alienated from us that we do not intend just another exploitation? We must remember that James Cone told us in 1969 that "any advice from whites to blacks on how to deal with white oppression is automatically under suspicion as a clever device to further enslavement" (Cone, 1969, 20).

Amilcar Cabral writes well of "the weapon of theory." His thesis is that the theories we learned in school are so used to guide and condition our thinking about strategy that we never raise them to consciousness to determine if they are themselves in error, even though they are the framework within which we operate our programs and set our directions. He was referring to Marx's theory of conflict according to which history is assumed to begin with surplus production. Following this thesis, nations of Africa that lived for centuries into modern times without that form of production would have to think of the centuries of their existence as prehistoric. In fact, however, it was during those centuries that the most sophisticated and dignified forms of social relations were being tried, developed, discarded and renewed. I mention this point here because some of the most promising models for non-hierarchical decision-making patterns come out of those "non-historical" societies. (Cabral)

There is a third kind of theory about human development in a social context that begins with the assumption that all peoples have a human range of gene-determined developmental potential which does not predetermine outcomes of human struggles for freedom; that particular cultures and historical moments are the product of the interaction of peoples with the same gene pool ranges but with differential access to human resources and faring differently with regard to the historical timings determining who gets control. This body of theory further assumes that those who invent and produce weapons have greater opportunity to capture and enslave peaceful peoples and to keep control over them. The theory does not assume that the making and use of weapons is a superior human act to negotiating with prior possessors of territory or resources as a means of sharing their needed resources (Lieberson, 1961). In fact, some who hold this theory unambiguously condemn those who choose to use weapons against other human beings.

Guided by this kind of theory, the history of the American Indians and the colonists gets rewritten and the enemies get allocated according to who intentionally attacked and destroyed the other for the purpose of stealing their possessions or destroying their people. According to this theory, it takes but the telling to condemn those who initiated the act of selling to unaware Indians blankets that had wrapped smallpox victims in the hope that this newly received disease would exterminate the tribe. And any held justification of this act on the basis of the

Social Darwinian principle of hastening the elimination of the non-saints is seen clearly for what it was, that is, the exploitative uses of communal religion, an act calling for atonement on the part of the sinning saints. Modern parallels of the smallpox act of the Massachusetts Bay colonists are to be found in the manner of handling the welfare system in a society that cannot provide jobs for five million of its employable workers yet is reluctant to provide welfare for its unemployed or even for its unemployables—making ability to work a contingency for existence in a world that does not need that work for effective production.

What Do "They" Want?

How do the poor, black, young and women feel about programs of reconciliation among all social groups? We cannot know unless we are told. Here is one powerful statement for our reflection. The speaker is Basil Moore, a South African theologian writing about Black theology. He is recounting the reaction of the English-speaking multi-racial churches to the introduction of the official apartheid program in South Africa in 1948. Prior to 1948, the English-background United Party had controlled the polity and the economy. In that setting the government enjoyed the support of the church despite its racism! Racism here refers to "a constant tendency on the part of whites to depict blacks as of an inferior status" (Moore, 1974, 42). After 1948, the government passed into the hands of the Afrikaaners —the descendants of the Dutch Boers—and so the English, though still controlling the economy, no longer controlled the government. At this point, the churches began encouraging multi-racial contact meetings. Moore makes these wry comments:

> Whatever the reasons for the rising tide of church-based opposition, it led to an increasing demand within the churches for multi-racialism. This of course was very limited. Little or no attempt was made within the churches to alter the white-dominated power structures of the churches.

All authority still resided in white hands. Whites continued to be appointed as bishops, general secretaries, etc., and continued to control financial concerns, publications and technological education (especially that of blacks). But alongside this white control arose the clamour for multi-racial contact. So there emerged a plethora of multi-racial meetings, synods, conferences, discussion or study groups, student movements, etc.

The religious rationale for this 'contact,' which also had its secular counterpart, was 'reconciliation.' Against the rising tide of racialism the churches or their leaders came to see the crucial need as being for 'reconciliation' between blacks and whites. This need for 'reconciliation' led to an almost pathological 'got-to-get-me-a-black-man-to-find-out-what-he-is-thinking' attitude among many whites.

The effects of this multi-racialism were not all negative. It is true that this 'reconciliation contact' did enable a few whites (very few) to move from their racialist inheritance to an open desire for non-racialism. But it is equally true that many more became rather sickening paternalists and charitable 'do-gooders.' Whether there were any positive effects on blacks in the multi-racialism is debatable. What is not debatable is that for blacks generally it was disastrous because it took place in the context of South African society, a society in which there is a vast gap in wealth and education between blacks and whites. In the main the whites who were ready, willing and able to enter into the 'dialogue' with blacks were highly educated and, even by white standards, wealthy. It was natural that the 'dialogue' they sought was with blacks who could more or less easily enter into their sophisticated discussion (i.e., that tiny upper-upper educated black elite) and whose standards of living compared favourably with their own (i.e., the tiny upper-upper economic black class).

As a consequence, the 'reconciliation' that took place was phony. What happened in effect was that 'class' loyalty took over from race loyalty. Black and white distinctions paled before the common bond of wealth and education (Moore, 1974, 2-4).

Today in South Africa there is a black resistance to multi-racialism. Perhaps the most significant factor that has made the emergence of Black theology possible in South Africa is the growing mood among Blacks against multi-racialism. I submit that this is a healthy orientation to be celebrated in the effort to realize the new Church mandate for reconciliation. I do not think the Spirit basis of reconciliation in the Church is in any way intended to try to break the growing power base of minority organization for realizing just demands for power and possessions. I think the Church in its stand expressed in *The Pastoral Constitution on the Church in the Modern World,* in *On the Development of Peoples,* in *Call to Action,* in the Synod of 1971 on Justice and Peace and now in the new document from the 1974 Synod intends to honor, support and encourage the mobilization for power-sharing on the part of the oppressed minorities of the world. This new recognition is that the powerlessness of the *anawim* which is reverenced in the biblical setting implies the affirmation of the right of existentially powerless peoples to take what rightfully belongs to them, since God has so affirmed their personhood that divine help will be theirs. As they reach out to the holders of the resources of the world to demand their share—a share equal to what a people needs to live in simple dignity with health, education and welfare services provided from the commonwealth and provided equally to all members according to their need—the rich are being asked to let go the firm grip they have developed in their interest, a grip embedded in the economy, polity, culture, science, education, art, philosophy and even in the theology that is celebrated in the Western world. The interests of the rich, white, older men of the world are organized politically, scientifically, culturally, economically, educationally and religiously to prevent the control of goods and services from passing from their hands. I do not think God blesses this privacy, this ascendancy, this assumption of righteousness, and this co-optation even of Christian ethics.

As people of the book, we are not called to reconciliation on the psychic level alone but are being challenged to reconciliation on the social level. We may still with felt reason fear and distrust groups different from our own. What we are being asked to do is to recognize that if those we fear and distrust have equal rights to survival with us then they also have equal rights to share in the planning about the disposal of resources. If they are systematically excluded from access to the resources of the world through law, culture, education and religious practice, then we can move toward reconciliation by helping change those laws, customs, education and religious practice and thus reduce the causes of fear and eliminate the bases of hate. We can then expect that not animals, not beasts, not supermen but people will be revealed to exist behind those facades that are raised against the enemy. We can then expect what from Scripture we hold as belief, that Christ came that all may have life and have it more abundantly. Thus, when some have in too great abundance, we can recognize this as evil and help to eliminate this evil by encouraging one another to let go as others reach out as our peers to grasp what is theirs.

We are not called to encourage the poor to turn on one another as they scramble over the scarce goods that are not sufficient for any group, nor to be reconciled with one another despite their shared deprivation. We are encouraged to help them to organize with greater strength, so that they can demand of those who really have the power and the resources their share of the common wealth. We are not called to siphon off the leaders of the oppressed, to break down their resistance to the powerful so that they cannot psychically brace themselves to express effectively the just demands of their people who are deprived. We are not called to blur the lines between the haves and the have-nots so that the people on the periphery are too confused to find the just causes in which they can freely invest their limited energies toward effective action. We are not called as Christians to do these destructive things. We do, however, often call ourselves to do them or respond to the call of our colleagues to do them, and it is frequently difficult, given the faces of Janus, to distinguish the calls. The wolves look so much like the sheep.

Conclusion

There is a great reconciliation to come when we struggle together to assure the poor, the Blacks, the young and the women that their health needs will be honored with the same concern that buys health care and choice of care today to the wealthiest man with the greatest power in our society. If we believe, as we say we do, in the right to life, then in the spirit of reconciliation we are going to use our energies to assure that health services of the finest type are available to those who are sick and maimed, not because they have status but because they have illnesses to be cured and are human beings with human rights. If white, male doctors, organized in the A.M.A., limit the opportunities for training of the unemployed and uneducated in the skills of much needed medical personnel, then in the spirit of reconciliation we are going to establish alternate medical centers to train professionals and para-professionals rapidly to develop public health programs in rural and crowded urban areas, local clinics at which all who have medical and dental needs can receive without cost the services required for human life. We are going to do this because in the spirit of reconciliation there is no other way to demonstrate that we really mean to reconcile. We who say we are Christian have no alternative if we have learned how easy it is to co-opt the Church to the paid-for interests of the powerful and the wealthy. Health, education and welfare have been our business since Christ healed the lame, cured the blind, raised the dead and taught the ignorant about rich men not getting into heaven until they have sold all they had, given it to the poor and come to follow him. But we have done that service for centuries by concentrating on patching up the effects of poverty. Recently, we have added another compromising skill to our repertoire, the crisis intervention that blurs the lines between oppressor and oppressed. Today we are called to a new approach to an age-old problem. It is a call to work on eliminating the causes of poverty rather than merely alleviating its results. This stance makes unambiguous what was unambiguous in Gospel days, that is, that the interests of the poor have primacy in Christian service. Conversion consists in taking this step to change our allegiance and to choose this stance. This is the issue around which there is polarization in the churches, between those who would perpetuate and those who would eliminate the institutions that cause poverty. The first position privatizes our religion and secularizes our politics; the second socializes our religion and humanizes our politics. Catholics and Evangelicals are polarizing on these alternatives, Catholics from Catholics, Evangelicals from Evangelicals. We have a rich resource of people to help direct us to truly biblical responses, people who are freer with regard to the system because the system is not organized in their interests. They are the poor, the Blacks, the young and the women.

6
Prophecy and the
Call to Action*

Within the past few years, and with accelerating speed, the prophetic function in the Judaeo-Christian tradition has come to merge its voice with that of the combined themes of the Old and New Left. Where the Old Left called for a redistribution of wealth and the New Left for a redistribution of power, the Pope's messages followed the same sequence from 1961 through 1971. The call for a redistribution of the world's wealth is found in John XXIII's *Mater et Magistra* which furthered the themes of Pius XI's *On the Reconstruction of the Social Order* (1931) and which introduced the focus for the *aggiornamento* of the Second Vatican Council on cultural and social restructuring. To those who had been following the Marxist tradition over the past hundred years these were not new themes; what was new was the espousal by the Catholic Church of these as its central concern. The Protestant churches had expressed this message earlier, through the World Council of Churches, but not with the same concerted emphasis and clarity.

The century-long struggle within the churches of the first world to affirm the legitimacy of basic changes in social structure, including the gamut of political, economic, class and cultural organization, reached a climax in Pope Paul VI's *Call to Action* in May 1971 (Paul VI, 1971a). The Roman Synod of November 1971 attempted some programming of this call to political participation, but it fell short of the implications of the

*Excerpted from "How Prophecy Lives," presidential address given at the annual meeting of the Association for the Sociology of Religion, New Orleans, La., August 27, 1972, and published in *Sociological Analysis* 33:3 (Fall, 1972).

Call itself, which focused the attention of the international church on the theme of justice in the world, the logical development of the deliberations of the Second Vatican Council (Abbott, 1966; Synod of Bishops, 1971). Paul VI's letter, addressed to Cardinal Roy as president of the Council of the Laity and of the Pontifical Commission on Justice and Peace, climaxed the eighty years of Catholic attempts to address a response to the social revolutions and to the prophets of those revolutions of the nineteenth and twentieth centuries. In his letter on the occasion of the eightieth anniversary of *Rerum Novarum* (Leo XIII, 1891), Pope Paul stated:

Under the driving force of new systems of production, national frontiers are breaking down, and we can see new economic powers emerging, multinational enterprises which by concentration and flexibility of their means can conduct autonomous strategies which are largely independent of the national political powers and therefore not subject to control from the point of view of the common good. By extending their activities, these private organizations can lead to a new and abusive form of economic domination on the social, cultural and even political level; the excessive concentration of means and powers that Pope Pius XI already condemned on the fortieth anniversary of *Rerum Novarum* is taking on a new and very real image (Paul VI, 1971a, #44).

And then, after adding a few significant details, he stated: "This is why the need is felt to pass from economics to politics" (#46). But he becomes even more specific regarding personal individual involvement in political action and says:

The passing to the political dimension also expresses a demand made by the man of today: A greater sharing in responsibility and decision-making. This legitimate aspiration becomes more evident as the cultural level rises, as the sense of freedom develops, and as man becomes more aware of how, in a world facing an uncertain future, the choices of today already condition the life of tomorrow. In *Mater et Magistra* Pope John XXIII stressed how much the admittance to responsibility is a basic demand of man's nature, a concrete exercise of his freedom, and a path to his development; and he showed how, in economic life and particularly in enterprise, this sharing in the responsibilities should be ensured. Today the field is wider and extends to the social and political sphere in which a reasonable sharing in responsibility and in decisions must be established and strengthened (#47).

After these words the Pope's rhetoric takes on a real prophetic cry as he says:

It is to all Christians that we address a fresh and insistent call to action. In our encyclical *On the Development of Peoples* we urged that all should set themselves the task [of] the renewal of the temporal order. It belongs to the laity, without waiting passively for orders and directives, to take the initiative freely and to infuse a Christian spirit into the mentality, customs, laws, and structures of the community in which they live. Let each one examine himself to see what he has done up to now, and what he ought to do. It is not enough to recall principles, state intentions, point to crying injustices, and utter prophetic denunciations; these words will lack real weight unless they are accompanied for each individual by a livelier awareness of personal responsibility and by effective action (#48).

The Pope was not speaking in the wilderness in 1971, but rather his voice was part of an orchestration begun in the nineteenth century and developing over the past eighty years in its papal form. Vatican Council II, in its struggles with meaning and modification, increased the clarity of this prophetic stance to a point where local churches and individuals could freely take an initiative and still feel that they were speaking in the spirit of the Council, even if they were not affirmed by ecclesiastical administrators. The test of the charism rested on three bases: (1) an effective address to third world oppression; (2) the actual involvement of the local community in the decisions that affected their lives; and (3) a recognition that this stand was rooted in the Gospels. (That the *Call to Action* is the result of prophetic influence can be seen in the light of the fact that, beginning in 1868, the Vatican had issued a series of decrees forbidding Italian Catholics from participating in parliamentary elections. Pope Pius IX initiated this policy during a period of uncertainty after the promulgation of the Constitution of the Kingdom of Italy in 1861. This was done because the government was hostile to the Church and especially to religious orders. The decree "Non Expedit" directed that there be no participation by Catholics in politics, either as "elector or elected." Besides having for a reason the principle that the oath taken by the deputies might be interpreted as an approval of the spoliation of the Holy See, a further reason was that "the masses seemed unprepared for parliamentary government"—U. Benigni, *Catholic Encyclopedia,* New York: Encyclopedia Press, Inc., 1911, XI, 98-99.)

The Medellín Conference of the Latin American bishops, working through numerous position papers toward the implementation of the decrees of Vatican II for Latin America, adopted in 1968 a policy directive of prophetic dimensions derived from the methods used in Brazil, Chile and elsewhere in Latin America, toward rapid basic education of the peasant not only to literacy but also to social, economic and political awareness. Conscientization is the name the process came to have, and it refers to "learning to perceive social, political and economic contradictions and to take action against the oppressive elements of reality" (Freire, 1970, 19), a method originally named and made popular through the action-reflection program of Paulo Freire, the brilliant teacher-scholar exile from Brazil, and his sponsor and friend Dom Helder Camara, Archbishop of Recife in northeast Brazil, both held in disrepute by the government now ruling Brazil, a government which has already attempted to co-opt the program to established interests (Freire, 1970).

In introducing their new stand the Latin American bishops said:

> We are at the beginning of a new historic epoch in our continent. It is filled with the hope of total emancipation—liberation from all servitude—personal maturity and collective integration. We foresee the painful gestation of a new civilization (Medellín Documents, 1970, I, 9).

And further:

> 'Medellín hurts because it demands radical changes and an abandoning of certain privileged positions,' Bishop Pironio explained. 'The Medellín commitment demands courage. Renovation also demands meditation and the sincere search for new roads. It would be dangerous to change for the sake of change, without understanding the significance and the demands of change' (*ibid.*).

Dom Avelar Brandao Vilela, president of CELAM, and the Secretary-General Eduardo F. Pironio made it clear that the conclusion of Medellín is in fact the expressed will of the assembled bishops. They state:

> The Documents contain the fruit of the labors of the sixteen commissions and sub-commissions into which the Conference was divided, and have been definitively approved by His Holiness Pope Paul VI (*ibid.*, 13).

They also assert:

> It will be well to note that different Congregations and Officers of the Roman Curia have had high praise for the texts submitted to their consideration (*ibid.*).

Further:

> The final Documents which we offer are the fruits of hard

work in productive intimacy with the Lord Jesus. They were fully developed at the fraternal sessions held in Medellín where the inspiration of the Holy Spirit was evident and responsible for gathering the bishops in the profound communion of the Church. We truly believe that in union with Mary, the Mother of Jesus, we lived an authentic Pentecost for the Latin American Church (*ibid.*).

These passages indicate the recognition by the leaders of the Conference that for them its product is holy.

In publishing the two volumes of the conference papers and conclusions, the Latin American Division of the United States Conference of Bishops includes this statement in the "Introduction and Dedication":

We have translated and published with CELAM the Medellín statements to facilitate the conscientization of English-speaking people of good will throughout the universal Church. A fuller understanding of the content and commitment of Medellín is the essential first step in the arduous task of seeking to actively implement these progressive pastoral guidelines (*ibid.*, 10).

A note that is not merely an appendage and is descriptive of part of the life of prophecy: Fr. Louis Michel Colonnese, editor of these papers and director of the Latin American Bureau and the one responsible for the publication of another volume on the same theme, *Conscientization and Liberation,* a volume dedicated to five Latin American prelates and to Paulo Freire, has since been fired by the Conference of Bishops because of a loss of "mutual trust and confidence between the staff person and the administration" (Bernardin, 1971).

In 1970 the Canadian Conference of Bishops in conjunction with the Canadian Council of Churches prepared for implementation a program derived from an affirmation of the Medellín documents that even more succinctly capsulized and affirmed the new direction mandated by Vatican II with this change of focus: "from the alleviation of the results of poverty to an elimination of its causes" (Canadian Conference of Bishops, 8). The specification that programs of social concern will be focused on the elimination of causes rather than alleviation of the results of poverty directs the prophetic message to action both on the deinstitutionalization of political, social and economic structures that are oppressive of the Third World and on the construction of whatever social forms are worked out by a membership reflecting and acting on its own oppressive situation in the process of conscientization (Medellín Documents, 1970, 65, 76, 81).

The life of prophecy in our times is illustrated by the stages of the Christian response to Karl Marx's charismatic condemnation of entrenched economic interest, a sequence ranging from repudiation to affirmation. There were the denials by the establishment, the attack on the prophetic voices, the rise of false prophets, the co-optation of prophecy. But there was also the struggle to free prophecy from entrenched power and interest, a growing awareness of what it means that religion is "the opium of the people," and an effort to replace the established content of socialization (so deeply mapped on the consciousness of church members) with the prophetic meaning, intention and action. When, despite the entrenched interests of their own positions, the established churches seriously examine oppressive social structures and then mandate action that is already meeting concerted resistance from that coalition of power and culture which serves transnational wealth, a new task is presented to students of the sociology of religion: to test seriously those hypotheses (far different from the hypotheses affirmed by established interests) that claim links between Christianity and socialism (*Latin America Calls,* 1972, 4-5). Even in the brief resume presented here one can begin to see that the new position of the Latin American church is radical, the Canadian church liberal, and the American church conservative. This gradation characterizes the degrees of power, wealth and control that the three geographical units have in the world economy.

Anchoring the recent life of prophecy in the cry of Marx is a proposal to be investigated. Like other prophets he made a serious denunciation of structured evil and placed considerable blame on religious institutions for providing an opium for the people. He located the causes of the existing structures in the social relations associated with the means of production, and in the control of consciousness to maintain effectively and develop that structure in the cultural carriers: family, education, recreation and religion. In elite control over violence and control of the unknown (mass media control) he saw the means of oppression. These themes repeatedly surface in sociological analysis today. I intend nothing more ideological than a plea that we examine why it is that the sociology of Marx is a crime against the state in South Africa, while that of Talcott Parsons is in the required curriculum of the state university social science program. I claim both scholars to be essential to sociological analysis and would be hard pressed to have to reject the one or the other in the study of social change and development.

Let us now turn to examine whether or not there is any evidence in the biblical tradition to suggest the shape of prophecy today in the transition to socialism (Sweezy and Bettleheim, 1971).

According to *The Jerome Biblical Commentary*, the prophet in biblical tradition stands in judgment on the nation. His task is the calling of his co-religionists to repent because their private and public lives belie the biblical message that they claim to be living. The Old Testament prophets were distinctly of Israel when they spoke "the fearless revelation of the moral will of Yahweh, the God of Israel's covenant" (p. 227). The prophet is called "one made to speak" (p. 225). A false prophet was not so much one who intended lies, but rather one who was so caught up in his own culture that he came to see Yahweh as willing what was in accord with Israel's preference, rather than reprimanding Israel when she acted out of line with Yahweh's will (p. 226). Prophets sat in judgment on the institutions of Israel and became the conscience of the nation (p. 227). This passing of judgment on the nation constituted a new role in the religions of the Near East, and has become part of the tradition of Western culture since that time (p. 229).

I am using prophecy in the biblical sense, distinguishing the role of the prophet from that of priest and wise man as did

Jeremiah, who divides the labor of religious role players with the priest fulfilling the law, the wise man taking the role of counselor, and the prophet speaking the Word of the Lord, that is, passing moral judgments on the behavior of the nation (Jeremiah 18:18). Bruce Vawter observes, however, that in the Old Testament times the prophets usually spoke in such a way that their hearers were led to make the most of existing institutions, rather than to exert the effort to change them. Rather than institutions, it was their own lives they tried to change (*The Jerome Biblical Commentary,* 1968, 231). They were occupied with concern for personal justice to the neighbor, with decrying the substitution of sacrifice for the seeking of forgiveness and making restitution, and particularly for the recognition of God as Father and Provider. They did, however, link social evil with sin. In fact, Second Isaiah does this quite eloquently when he says:

> Will you call this a fast
>   and a day acceptable to the Lord?
> Is not the fast that I choose:
>   to loose the bonds of wickedness,
>   to undo the thongs of the yoke,
>   to let the oppressed go free
>   and to break every yoke?
> Is it not to share your bread with the hungry and bring the
>   homeless poor into your house;
> When you seek the naked, to cover him,
>   and not to hide yourself from your own flesh?
> Then shall your light break forth like the dawn
>   and your healing shall spring up speedily.
> Your righteousness shall go before you,
>   the glory of the Lord shall be your rear guard.
> Then you shall call, and the Lord will answer;
>   you shall cry, and he will say, here I am (Isaiah 58:5-
>   9).

The commentary on this passage in *The Jerome Biblical Commentary* suggests that this type passage in the Old Testament may be a call not for social justice but rather for personal justice to the individual captive or oppressed person. It notes as evidence of this the existence of cult and court prophets as in other religions of the Near East—that is, those who affirmed the culture and power of legitimate rulers. It notes further that even ecstasy was associated with prophecy, hinting that prophecy included the experience of indifference toward the conditions of this world and the directive to seek escape from it, a type of prophecy also common to other religions. However, as Vawter clearly points out, what distinguished biblical prophecy from that of any other nation of that time was the emphasis on social morality, and that this and not the call either to court prophecy or to ecstasy was the main characteristic of the biblical prophet. He says in part:

> They (that is, the prophets) were only insisting on the social virtues inherent in the doctrines of election, virtues which had been flagrantly violated in an Israel that had largely abandoned its ancient ideals by assimilating itself to Gentile ways. In pressing the social character of the religion of Yahweh, the prophets were proposing nothing new but recalling a known, although much ignored, morality. . . .

> Poverty was never sentimentalized by the prophets of Israel; in keeping with the rest of the Old Testament, it was regarded as an undesirable thing. The poor man was not just because he was poor, but the existential fact could not be ignored that poverty and injustice were frequent companions. It was the evil of other men that had created this situation and the whole prophetic effort was directed against this evil (*The Jerome Biblical Commentary,* 233).

Vawter notes that this theme also extends to the New Testament. The New Testament prophetic voices are those of John the Baptist and Christ himself (Matthew 11:7-15), and they reiterate the demand to repent and to "bear fruit that befits repentance," disclaiming any hope of salvation merely because one belongs—that is, because one is a son of Abraham. John called his brethren a "brood of vipers" and warned them of the wrath to come unless they repented. But when they begged to know "What then shall we do?" he answered them: "He who has two coats, let him share with him who has none; and he who has food, let him do likewise" (Luke 3:8-11). Christ continued this theme by promising the Kingdom to the poor (Matthew 5:3). Current prophetic voices get their leverage from this Gospel root, and scholarly church research of the most recent years disaffirms any rationalization that tries to claim that this promising the Kingdom to the poor in spirit includes the rich who are "spiritually detached" from their wealth. *The Jerome Biblical Commentary,* in treating both prophecy and the Beatitudes, disclaims that the Kingdom is promised by Christ to anyone but the materially poor *(The Jerome Biblical Commentary,* 1968, I, 233; II, 70).

Who are the prophets today in the Judaeo-Christian tradition of prophecy? To answer the question we have to find those who cry out against injustice and seriously chide established interests, those who are rich and those whose task it is to enforce the law despite its demonstrated quality of institutionalized oppression. Further, we must look for those who in doing this act of biblical justice are inveighed against, attacked in character, allowed no public forum by the existing powers and who, though found to be credible by the oppressed themselves, are publicly suspect as subversive and privately viewed by their colleagues who are financially secure or relatively safe in the system as demented, naive, foolish, dangerous and evil. One further point, however, is that what they are saying must be in line with the Gospel, even though their personal lives are reported as at least maverick in quality and at most immoral from the point of view of the system. Given this criterion, we can include Philip and Daniel Berrigan, and the Catonsville nine, Milwaukee fourteen and other witnesses to peace, and define their behavior as prophetic witness. We can include Mahatma Gandhi, and his disciples for non-violence, Martin Luther King and Dom Helder Camara, all but one of whom were familiar with the inside of jail and one with death by violence, as prophets of action. We can include Frantz Fanon and Paulo Freire, both products of third world culture and first world professional training, who experienced exile as punishment for their teaching although that teaching was internationally recognized as humane and Christian. We can include as prophets of the word Cosmas Desmond, O.S.F., Ernest Cole, Govan Mbeke and Chief Albert J. Luthuli, all of South Africa, who, though recognized internationally for the human compassion of their denunciations, have suffered exile, house arrest and curtailment of their careers as punishment by their government for revealing its structured evil. Cesar Chavez, Angela Davis and George Jackson by the witness of their lives and their writings have been recognized as holy by the oppressed and as evil by the system. Today the man whose life best expresses the prophetic stance is Amilcar Cabral, a scholar who did yeoman work in standing with the people as they moved to freedom (Cabral, 1969); and the woman, her work still obscured by the impact of her word, Mary Daly (Daly, 1973). But if we include these and the many others who speak for the oppressed poor, then we have to include Karl Marx, whose cry of condemnation regarding religion was so pervasive that the meaning of what he said was obscured for one hundred years, so violent was the reaction of the established systems to a serious consideration of his word. Only in our time is it safe to name him as prophet and only because his message is in some respects indistinguishable from that of the priest. Listen to these priestly words:

> Capitalism has often bred too much misery, too much injustice, too much bitterness and strife. Industrialization itself has not brought these abuses. The wretched system that came along with it has brought evil into being (Paul VI, 1968, #26).

> The earth's goods must be divided fairly and this right of every man to a just share comes first. Even the right to private property and the right to free enterprise must yield to justice. All other rights must help, not block, this basic right of every man (#22).

> From time to time the good of all demands that private property should be taken over by the state. This should be

done if landed estates have grown too great or cause dire poverty; or if they hamper seriously the prosperity of the whole community (#24).

Left to itself the workings of international trade tend to make the rich richer, while the poor develop slowly if at all (#8).

Between May and August of 1971 I have read these quotations to groups of Catholics—in Boston, for religious educators; in North Dartmouth, Massachusetts, for major superiors of men's and women's orders; in Chicago, for a similar group; in North Dartmouth again in 1972, for sixty-five Catholic school superintendents; in Rhodesia, for religious educators; in South Africa, for bishops, religious and lay religious teachers in ten different areas; and during this summer for religious men and women in New York, Maryland and Boston again. In every case, from not more than ten people in audiences ranging from fifty to over a thousand can I get an affirmation that these are Gospel words. Each group senses their similarity to principles they believe to be associated only with dialectical materialism and hence to be rejected by Gospel followers, and yet they are *verbatim* from the present Pontiff's encyclical *On the Development of Peoples.*

7
Toward a Theology
of Relinquishment*

For many centuries, people who wrote about society tended
to think in terms of elites and masses—that is, in terms of a
two-class system, of which one class included planners, administrators, designers and directors, and the other the mass of labor-
ers, clerical assistants and the poor. Of the poor, some were la-
borers but others so poor that they were merely the
dispossessed, foraging for life like animals because lacking the
necessities for survival with dignity. Religious people cared for
them, mostly helping them to prepare for a good death with the
expectation that at least in eternity they would be at peace (De
Castro, 1969). Through religious systems, law systems developed, beginning from a basis in the *paterfamilias* of Roman law
(protecting the rights of fathers over wives, children and slaves),
developing in turn the divine rights of kings, then civil rights
and finally human rights. Through religious influence as well as
economic necessity, health services and educational training
were extended to citizens as more workers were needed in production units. With health and education there developed evidence that the masses are not really masses at all but people,
people who have inadequate space for living and hence experience the deterioration of their human potential, an experience
deadening to the spirit when people are powerless to change it.
This discovery—that in a humane environment people develop
their human potential because there is psychic space for the
emergence of new consciousness—permitted the formation of

*Paper presented at Religious Studies Institute: "Challenges for the Con-
temporary Christian," College of Notre Dame, Baltimore, Md., May 1, 1976.

103

self-conscious groups demanding the share of the world's resources belonging to them by reason of their human rights.
Even though religious people often helped in this group development, religious systems adapted to the old pattern of the
noblesse oblige of the elite failed to notice this change in the
consciousness of people—especially, unfortunately, if some religious people made their own living by "helping the poor." What
we now know is that people for whom the existence of poor people is a requisite of their profession—including ministers of the
Gospel, medical personnel, funeral directors, judges, teachers,
welfare workers, psychologists, civil servants, military and police personnel—can, unless they are continually made aware of
the personhood of the poor, actually insist on the existence of
less-than-human qualities in poor people in order to assure their
own job continuity, and thus become instrumental in keeping
the poor people down (Piven, 1971; "If There Were No Black
People We Would Have To Invent Them," Impact Films, New
York). It is hard for us to accept that observation as anything
more than trivial distortion. I am presenting it as a serious
hypothesis worthy of pursuit and in fact already the subject of
serious research (Piven; Ryan). Were we not in such dire need
of a profession to sustain our standard of living we professionals
would not need to develop the blindness that helps to continue
the manifest injustice that clearly calls for alternatives as the
poor, newly conscious of their rights and capacities, claim what
is rightfully theirs, including the same serious training in skills
that has long been accorded the non-poor in the helping and
other professions. The poor are seeking self-help and this is
being resisted even by those trained to help them.

What is called for on the part of the non-poor is relinquishment. Relinquishment has always been called for by the Gospel,
but it has frequently been resisted or else cast in individualistic
terms because we have no theology of relinquishment. Today,
with the growing affirmation of a theology of liberation by the
poor, we need a corresponding method, peculiar to the non-
poor, to think about God. The reason is that today the situation
is different from formerly. When the poor rise to claim what
belongs to them, as they are now doing, we need to know what

the Gospel directs the non-poor to do. The evidence is persuasive.

First, the Gospel mandates the poor to take what is theirs.
Pope Paul VI, writing in *On the Development of Peoples*
(1967), indicates with a reference to St. Ambrose, one of the
early Church Fathers, that when the rich give the poor what
they ask for they are only giving them what is already theirs
(#22). Whence comes this right to possession? In Leviticus 25:1-
10 and 25-28, God tells Moses to announce to the heads of state
that they are to decree every fiftieth year a year of jubilee, a
year in which whatever property people have lost for whatever
reason—whether it be by sale, in payment for a debt, by revolution, etc.—is to be returned to them. They or their families are
to pay for it if they have resources; otherwise, in the fiftieth
year, those holding the land are to return it anyway. This clearly indicates that land cannot be alienated from the people in
perpetuity. In a crowded world we can certainly interpret that
today to mean that people have a right to the disposal of the
resources of the land where they live. In Deuteronomy 24:10, in
a discussion of loans, there is a clear explanation that whatever
a person pledges for a loan is to be returned before sundown if
the person needs it for the night. The example used is that of a
poor person's cloak. What is made clear is that no right of own-
ership supersedes human need. Because the hungry soldiers were
allowed to eat the loaves of proposition reserved for temple
worship, and the apostles the corn in a private cornfield on the
sabbath, we know clearly that no matter who possesses food it
belongs to hungry peoples. Relinquishing one's claim to what
others need is clearly a Gospel mandate. The claim is not sup-
posed to be relinquished foolishly, as some have argued, in such
a way that Christianity becomes an impossible ideal. The obli-
gation is one of justice, to be honored when the society fails to
provide for its members and for sojourners. The point is that
the resources of society belong to the people. People who violate
just laws, on the other hand, are to be punished.

The extent of the biblical mandate is even more explicit in
the New Testament. Here the distinction, so carefully drawn in
Leviticus and other Old Testament passages, between slaves and

free people, between heads of households and their wives, is eliminated in Galatians 3:28, which indicates that, in the application of Christian doctrine, no distinction is to be made on the basis of being Jew or Gentile, slave or free, male or female. In Luke and Mark the New Testament is very explicit in teaching that the rich can reach perfection only by selling their riches, giving to the poor and following Jesus (Mark 10:17-23; Luke 19:18-30). Moreover, Jesus declares here that it is easier for a camel to get through the eye of a needle than for a rich man to enter heaven. The astonished reaction of his followers to this statement is answered by Jesus with the remark that what is impossible with human beings is possible with God. Many people interpret that to mean that God can manage to get the rich into heaven, an explanation that contradicts and wastes the Gospel. It is more accurate to say that the utopian society Jesus proclaims in which the rich will actually give up their goods, though impossible for human beings to achieve on their own, can be achieved with the help of God. That, I think, is the great hope of today.

We have seen the two large experiments in socialism in the Soviet Union and in China accomplish what we had believed could not be accomplished—the elimination of basic poverty and the provision of medical services and care in retirement for the people. This seems to be better programmed in China than in Russia, and to have been accomplished there with much less destruction of human life. Marx believed that violent revolution is always necessary when wresting power from those who control the resources of society, since no one gives it up willingly. The violence occurs because of the exploitation prior to the day of accounting and the resistance to its correction. The history of Rhodesia and South Africa since 1948 provides examples. These two Christian countries and the European countries from which the white populations originated have resisted sharing power with those from whom they wrested the land by force of arms until threatened by force of arms themselves. As Americans, we do the very same thing at home and abroad. As Christians, we come thereby under the judgment of the Gospel. As human beings, we are free to ignore the judgment or to respond to it; though if we ignore it, we are responsible for the effect of our decision on human society. While the Gospel calls on the poor to take what they need, the non-poor are called to repentance, which consists in giving away one's second coat and food to those who have none (Luke 3:1-11). This clearly indicates that repentance is directly associated with restoring goods to the poor. Sin, accordingly, must be associated with retaining goods that the poor need for their survival. Many Westerners look at the Eastern experiments with socialism and declare that the price in human destruction has been too high. People exiled from those societies object strongly to the fact that they lost their goods. What the words of the Gospel seem to mean is that, by not repudiating the Gospel as Marx did or reinterpreting it as the non-poor have done, a society that provides for the people could be attained without violence, because the repentant Christian would be required to share resources with those who have none. That we do not see this as part of the Christian mandate is overwhelmingly evident in our lack of knowledge of where the very poor are even located, whether they be in our own cities or in the other nations of the world. We scarcely know the reality of poverty. Even when we do see real poverty, we account for it in terms of poor administration in those countries or cities, as if that canceled out the mandate to eliminate it. It is clear in Leviticus that, regardless of the causes of loss of property, it still is to be given back to the people. In Gospel terms, the sole determinant of the right to possession is human need. No rationale explaining the reason that poverty exists is an adequate substitute for the Christian task of eliminating it. This is a larger task than can be accomplished with private charity. It is a task of public planning. For this reason, those Christians shy away from it who have been trained in individualistic or personalist religious responses to the established economic system.

The reason that most Christian ministers are from the working class is probably explained by the story of the rich man who wanted to be perfect but turned away because he had vast possessions. He turned away sadly, it is true, and Jesus yet loved him, but he did not in fact follow Jesus (Luke 19:18-32).

It is hard for the rich to give up possessions. By the same token, it is easy for me to preach this Gospel because I do not have many possessions. But Jesus did not say that one can preach relinquishment of riches only if one has them. All the apostles were poor. Hard or easy to do, in the Christian context the wealth belongs to the people and no one is justified in wealth while some are dispossessed. What constitutes the good news to the poor that the Gospel is said to be but this, that they are to possess the land (Luke 6:30)? Many scriptural passages indicate the task for Christians. The judgment of the nations, for example, rests on giving to the hungry, welcoming the stranger, clothing the naked, caring for the sick, visiting those in prison— not as side issues, but as a life work. It is on these bases that the sheep are separated from the goats on the day of atonement (Matthew 25:31-46). In the Magnificat, Mary cried out joyfully that the poor would be filled and the rich sent away empty (Luke 1:46-55). The rich man who was in hell because he ignored the beggar Lazarus at his table was told that all his brothers needed to do to save their lives was to listen to Moses and the prophets telling them to feed the beggar (Luke 16:19-31). Personal holiness and the judgment of nations are equally related to providing for the poor all that is needed for their lives. Love of neighbor is described as helping the poor and despoliated neighbor whom the priest and levite might ignore (Luke 10:25-37). Two years ago, when the Brazilian bishops announced to the world that they had "heard the cries of their people," they quoted 1 John 3:17-18: "But if anyone has the world's goods and sees his brother in need, yet closes his heart against him, how does God's love abide in him?" Lest his listeners take him to mean that we ought to love the poor *despite* their poverty, John adds: "Let us not love in word or speech but in deed and in truth." Our own U.S. bishops, including the head of the U.S. Bishops' Conference, in their proclamation "This Land Is Home to Me," use this scriptural passage to justify the people's rights to the land and to public services (Bernardin, *et al.,* 1975). In case the rich should think that in giving away their goods they would be deprived of sustenance, the Gospel gives assurance that by heeding its mandate all will have more and the Kingdom will come. Back in the days of Isaiah this was the promise, as this fiery prophet called for a return of justice to the land:

.The afflicted and the needy seek water in vain,
    their tongues are parched with thirst.
I, the Lord, will answer them;
    I, the God of Israel, will not forsake them.
I will open up rivers on the bare heights,
    and fountains in the broad valleys;
I will turn the desert into a marshland,
    and the dry ground into springs of water.
I will plant in the desert the cedar,
    acacia, myrtle, and olive;
I will set in the wasteland the cypress,
    together with the plane tree and the pine,
That all may see and know,
    observe and understand,
That the hand of the Lord has done this,
    the Holy One of Israel has created it (Isaiah 41:17-20).

Moreover, we all await the promised land described in Isaiah 65. However, we have been so afraid to attempt this task for fear the Lord will not be with us—that we will be deserted and without possessions—that we have left it to the non-believer to show us the way. Now it is time for us to follow their lead, but with a difference. With a theology of relinquishment, derived from Scripture, in response to the theology of liberation that provides the poor with a method for reflecting on the conditions of their lives and for taking action to eliminate the oppressions they experience, the non-poor would have available some formal direction in preparing themselves for a spontaneous response to the rising poor of the world, a non-violent response on account of the Gospel mandate to release our grip on the resources as the poor reach out for them. The Eucharist is the sign that the food will be multiplied so that we all can eat (Mark 8:11-21). We are assured that if we lose our lives we will save them (Mark 8:34-35), and that if we sell all and give we will have treasure in heaven (Luke 12:33). We have been telling the poor for centuries that their reward will be in heaven. We are only being asked to believe what we have preached as good news to them (Weber, 1963, chapters VI, VII, VIII). The apostle Paul prided himself on working with his hands for a living and preaching in the evening (Acts 20:33-35), and Isaiah promised that the Lord will help the workers of the world in their task of building the kingdom in which peace will reign (Isaiah 65).

Should all this sound too utopian, Leviticus, in announcing the jubilee, also announced how to prepare for it by the sabbatical year every seven years. Because God knew it would be hard for us to refrain from accumulating more than we need for adequate living, the sabbatical was recommended for all adults. In this seventh year, which could be programmed for the four billion people who live in our society, about fourteen percent of the adults could be on sabbatical each year. The purpose of the year is to cease from customary activity—whether it be caring for children, tilling the soil, construction work, clerical work, teaching, medicine, or being unemployed—to review our lives and to decide whether we should continue in the same way of life for the next seven years. With a little imagination and vision we can see that, given this sabbatical, rich and poor alike could have time for public service, for visiting those in prisons and those who are ill, for doing jury duty, for attending public hearings and sustaining the quality of justice in the land, for learning about the peoples of the world, for improving competence in our chosen career, for doing the public and private tasks of reflection. How would one live in that year? On the commonwealth—on what we now call public welfare. Such an arrangement would have many benefits. It would free up several million jobs, reducing or even eliminating the high unemployment rate. It would reduce job security and allow people to develop a more flexible attitude toward changing jobs. It would make many more people interested in the quality of public housing, medical services and other welfare services, since they would be living on them every seventh year. What sounds utopian becomes, if one thinks of the problems of poverty and the need of human services in world perspective, a pragmatic need. In theological perspective, it has enormous potential for humanizing, energizing and tapping the creative imagination of a people close to anomie and alienation. The planning and developing of resources is a task for all the people and the construction of social, political and economic systems that provide effectively for human need is a Christian responsibility. It is the function of the church to provide a vision and tools for reflection commensurate to this task. These reflections, then, are offered as an invitation to the theologians, who take the Gospel seriously and are grasped by its vision, to shape the tools for reflection that will stir us to the action the Gospel demands.

Bibliography

Abbott, Walter M., ed., *The Documents of Vatican II.* New York: Guild Press, 1966

Ahlstrom, Sidney, *A Religious History of the American People.* New Haven: Yale Univ. Press, 1972

Allport, Gordon, *The Nature of Prejudice.* New York: Doubleday, 1958

Antoine, Charles, *Church and Power in Brazil.* Maryknoll, N.Y.: Orbis, 1973

Arroyo, Gonzalo, *Christians for Socialism: A Christian Response.* New York: IDOC - North America, No. 53 (May, 1971)

Barnet, Richard, and Ronald Müller, "Reporter at Large: Global Reach," in two parts, in *The New Yorker,* December 2 and 9, 1974. These are lengthy excerpts from *Global Reach* (New York: Simon and Schuster, 1975)

Baum, Gregory, *The Credibility of the Church Today.* New York: Herder and Herder, 1968

Bell, Daniel, "Religion in the Sixties," *Social Research,* XXXVIII (1971), 447-497

Bellah, Robert N., *Beyond Belief: Essays on Religion in a Post-Traditional World.* New York: Harper and Row, 1970

Bellah, Robert N., "American Civil Religion in the 1970's," *Anglican Theological Review,* Supplementary Series 1 (July, 1973), 8-20

Bellah, Robert N., *The Broken Covenant: American Civil Religion in Time of Trial.* New York: Seabury, 1975

Berger, Peter L., *The Sacred Canopy: Elements of a Sociological Theory of Religion.* New York: Doubleday (Anchor), 1967

Berger, Peter L., and Thomas Luckmann, *The Social Construction of Reality: A Treatise on the Sociology of Knowledge.* New York: Doubleday (Anchor), 1967

Bernardin, J., "Colonnese's Dismissal," IDOC - North America 34:30-31, New York, 1971

Bernardin, Joseph L., *et al.,* "This Land Is Home to Me: A Pastoral Letter on Powerlessness in Appalachia by the Catholic Bishops of the Region," February 1, 1975. *The Catholic Virginian,* February 21, 1975, 8-A

Brazilian Bishops, "I Hear the Cries of My People," IDOC - North America 54 (1973), New York

112

Brown, Michael B., *The Economics of Imperialism.* Baltimore: Penguin, 1974

Brown, Robert McAfee, *Frontiers of the Church Today.* New York: Oxford University Press, 1971

Cabral, Amilcar, *Revolution in Guinea: Selected Texts of Amilcar Cabral.* Ed. and trans. Richard Handyside. New York: Monthly Review Press, 1969

Camara, Dom Helder, *Spiral of Violence.* Denville, N.J.: Dimension, 1971

Canadian Conference of Bishops, "Towards a Coalition for Development," Strategy Committee Report, 1969

Caplowitz, David, *The Poor Pay More.* New York: Free Press, 1967

Cole, E., *House of Bondage.* New York: Random House, 1967

Colonnese, Louis M., ed., *Conscientization for Liberation.* Washington, D.C.: United States Catholic Conference, 1971

Cone, James H., *Black Theology and Black Power.* New York: Seabury, 1969

Daly, Mary, *Beyond God the Father.* Boston: Beacon, 1973

Dawson, Christopher, *Religion and Culture.* New York: Sheed and Ward, 1948.

De Castro, Josue, *Death in the Northeast: Poverty and Revolution in the Northeast of Brazil.* New York: Random House (Vintage), 1969

Desmond, Cosmas, *The Discarded People: An Account of African Resettlement in South Africa.* Baltimore: Penguin, 1971

"Dom Helder Camara Denounces," Brazilian Information Service, No. 7 (May, 1972)

Douglas, Mary, *Natural Symbols.* New York: Random House, 1972

Douglas, Mary, ed., *Rules and Meanings.* London: Penguin, 1973

Dowd, Douglas, *The Twisted Dream: Capitalist Development in the United States since 1776.* Cambridge, Mass.: Winthrop, 1974

Durkheim, Emile, *The Division of Labor.* Glencoe, Ill.: Free Press, 1953

Durkheim, Emile, *The Elementary Forms of the Religious Life.* New York: Free Press, 1965 (Orig. pub. 1915)

Eagleson, John, ed., *Christians and Socialism: Documentation of the Christians for Socialism Movement.* Maryknoll, N.Y.: Orbis, 1975

Fanon, Frantz, *The Wretched of the Earth.* New York: Grove, 1963

Fanon, Frantz, *Black Skins, White Masks.* New York: Grove, 1967 (Orig. pub. 1952)

Fenn, Richard K., "A New Sociology of Religion," *Journal for the Scientific Study of Religion* 2 (March, 1972), 16-32

Frazier, E. Franklin, and Eric Lincoln, *The Negro Church in America; The Black Church since Frazier.* New York: Schocken, 1963

Freire, Paulo, *Pedagogy of the Oppressed.* Trans. Myra B. Ramos. New York: Herder and Herder, 1970

Freud, Sigmund, *The Future of an Illusion*. New York: Liveright, 1949

Freud, Sigmund, *Civilization and Its Discontents*. New York: Norton, 1962

Gallup, George, "Religion in America," Opinion Index: Report No. 114, 1975

Geertz, Clifford, "Religion as a Cultural System," in *Anthropological Approaches to the Study of Religion*, ed. Michael Banton. London: Tavistock, 1966, 1-46

Gilkey, Langdon, *Naming the Whirlwind: The Renewal of God-Language*. Indianapolis: Bobbs-Merrill, 1969

Glazer, Nathan, *American Judaism*. Chicago: Univ. of Chicago Press, 1972

Glock, Charles Y., and Ellen Siegelman, *Prejudice U.S.A.* New York: Praeger, 1969

Glock, Charles Y., and Rodney Stark, *Religion and Society in Tension*. Chicago: Rand McNally, 1965

Goulet, D., and M. Hudson, *The Myth of Aid*. New York: IDOC - North America, 1973

Greeley, Andrew M., *The Denominational Society: A Sociological Approach to Religion in America*. Glenview, Ill.: Scott, Foresman, 1972

Greeley, Andrew M., *Ethnicity in the United States: A Preliminary Reconnaissance*. New York: Wiley, 1974

Greene, Felix, *The Enemy: What Every American Should Know About Imperialism*. New York: Random House (Vintage), 1970

Gutiérrez, Gustavo, *A Theology of Liberation: History, Politics and Salvation*. Maryknoll, N.Y.: Orbis, 1973

Hadden, Jeffrey, *The Gathering Storm in the Churches: A Sociologist Looks at the Widening Gap between Clergy and Laymen*. New York: Doubleday (Anchor), 1969

Harrington, Michael, *The Other America: Poverty in the United States*. Baltimore: Penguin, 1967

Harrington, Michael, *Socialism*. New York: Bantam, 1973

Hartford Statement, "An Appeal for Theological Affirmation." See *The New York Times*, March 9, 1975, for a report of the January meeting of eighteen ecumenists seeking a more theological basis for social action, having found the social movements of the 1960's too secular.

Hegel, G. W. F., *Reason in History: A General Introduction to the Philosophy of History*. Trans. Robert Hartmann. Indianapolis: Bobbs-Merrill, 1953

Herberg, Will, *Protestant, Catholic, Jew*. New York: Doubleday, 1960

Hinton, William, *Fanshen*. New York: Random House (Vintage), 1968

Homans, George, "Social Behavior as Exchange," *American Journal of Sociology* 62 (1958)

Homans, George, *Social Behavior: Its Elementary Forms*. New York: Harcourt, Brace, Jovanovitch, 1974

IDOC, an international documentary service, International Documentation Center, Rome, Italy

Jerome Biblical Commentary. Englewood Cliffs, N.J.: Prentice Hall, 1968. "Prophecy," 223-237; "Beatitudes," 62-114

John XXIII, *Mother and Teacher (Mater et Magistra).* New York: America Press, 1961

John XXIII, *Peace on Earth (Pacem in Terris).* New York: America Press, 1964

Jones, William R., *Is God a White Racist? A Preamble to Black Theology.* New York: Doubleday, 1973

Kanter, Rosabeth M., *Commitment and Community: Communes and Utopias in Sociological Perspective.* Cambridge, Mass.: Harvard University Press, 1972

Kapungu, Leonard T., *Rhodesia: The Struggle for Freedom.* Maryknoll, N.Y.: Orbis, 1974

Kaufman, Gordon, *God the Problem.* Cambridge, Mass.: Harvard Univ. Press, 1972

Kelley, Dean, *Why Conservative Churches are Growing.* New York: Harper and Row, 1972

Knox, Ronald A., *Enthusiasm: A Chapter in the History of Religion.* Oxford: Clarendon Press, 1950

LADOC (Latin American Documentation), a series published by the Division for Latin America of the United States Catholic Conference, Washington, D.C.; this publication comes out six times a year and provides documents of the efforts towards social justice in all the Latin American countries

Larson, Calvin J., *Major Themes in Sociological Theory.* New York: David McKay, 1973

Latin America Calls. Washington, D.C.: United States Catholic Conference, 1972

"Latin Americans Discuss Marxism-Socialism," LADOC. Washington, D.C.: United States Catholic Conference, 1975

Lenski, Gerhard, *The Religious Factor: A Sociological Study of Religion's Impact on Politics, Economics and Family Life.* New York: Doubleday (Anchor), 1963

Leo XIII, "The Condition of Labor" (*Rerum Novarum,* 1891), in *Four Great Encyclicals,* N.Y.: Paulist Press, 1961

Lieberson, Stanley, "A Societal Theory of Race and Ethnic Relations," *American Sociological* Review, December, 1961

Lincoln, Eric, ed., *The Black Experience in Religion: A Book of Readings.* New York: Doubleday (Anchor), 1974

Luckmann, Thomas, *The Invisible Religion: The Transformation of Symbols in Industrial Society.* New York: Macmillan, 1967

Machiavelli, N., *The Prince.* New York: Scribner, 1953

Magdoff, H., *The Age of Imperialism: The Economics of U.S. Foreign Policy.* New York: Monthly Review Press, 1969

Marty, Martin, "The Persistence of the Mystical," *Concilium,* New Series 1. Eds. Andrew Greeley and Gregory Baum. New York: Herder and Herder, 1973a, 36-45

Marty, Martin, *The Fire We Can Light: The Role of Religion in a Suddenly Different World.* New York: Doubleday, 1973b

Marty, Martin, *Protestantism: Its Churches and Cultures, Rituals and Doctrines, Yesterday and Today.* Garden City, N.Y.: Doubleday (Image), 1974

Marx, Karl, and Friedrich Engels, *Basic Writings on Politics and Philosophy,* ed. Lewis S. Feuer. New York: Doubleday (Anchor), 1959

Mbeke, Govan, *South Africa: The Peasants' Revolt.* Baltimore: Penguin, 1964

McBrien, Richard P., *The Remaking of the Church.* New York: Harper and Row, 1973

MacCarthy, Esther, "The Catholic Periodical Press and Issues of War and Peace, 1914-1946." Stanford University Doctoral Thesis, 1977

McKenzie, John L., "The Gospel According to Matthew," *The Jerome Biblical Commentary.* Englewood Cliffs, N.J.: Prentice Hall, 1968, II, 69-71

McNamara, Patrick H., ed., *Religion American Style.* New York: Harper and Row, 1974

Medellín Documents. *The Church in the Present Day Transformation of Latin America in the Light of the Council.* Official English edition. Washington, D.C.: United States Catholic Conference, and Bogotá, Colombia: Latin American Episcopal Council, 1970

Míguez Bonino, José, *Doing Theology in a Revolutionary Situation.* Philadelphia: Fortress, 1975

Moberg, David O., *The Great Reversal: Evangelism Versus Social Concern,* Philadelphia: Lippincott, 1972

Moodie, T. Dunbar, *The Rise of Afrikanerdom: Power, Apartheid and Afrikaner Civil Religion.* Berkeley: Univ. of California Press, 1975

Moore, Basil, ed., *The Challenge of Black Theology in South Africa,* Atlanta, Ga.: John Knox Press, 1974

Neal, Marie Augusta, S.N.D.deN., *Values and Interests in Social Change.* Englewood Cliffs, N.J.: Prentice Hall, 1965

Nozick, Robert, *Anarchy, State and Utopia.* New York: Basic Books, 1975

O'Brien, David J., *The Renewal of American Catholicism.* New York: Oxford Univ. Press, 1972

Parsons, Talcott, *The System of Modern Societies.* Englewood Cliffs, N.J.: Prentice Hall, 1971

Paul VI, *On the Development of Peoples.* Boston: St. Paul Editions, 1967

Paul VI, *The Development of Peoples,* creative trans. R. V. Bogan. Chicago: Claretian Publications, 1968

Paul VI, *A Call to Action,* Apostolic Letter on the Eightieth Anniversary of *Rerum Novarum.* Washington, D.C.: United States Catholic Conference, 1971a

Pettigrew, Thomas and Ernest Campbell, *Christians in Racial Crisis.* Washington, D.C.: Public Affairs Press, 1959

Pius XI, "On the Reconstruction of the Social Order (*Quadragesimo Anno,* 1931)," in *Four Great Encyclicals,* N.Y.: Paulist Press, 1961

Piven, Frances Fox, and Richard A. Cloward, *Regulating the Poor: The Functions of Public Welfare.* New York: Pantheon, 1971

Piven, Frances Fox, and Richard A. Cloward, *The Politics of Turmoil: Essays on Poverty, Race and the Urban Crisis.* New York: Pantheon, 1974

Pope, Liston, "Religion and Class Structure," *Annals of the American Academy of Political and Social Science,* 256 (1949)

Richey, Russell E. and Donald G. Jones, eds., *American Civil Religion.* New York: Harper and Row, 1974

Ruether, Rosemary, *Religion and Sexism: Images of Women in the Judaeo-Christian Theological Tradition.* New York: Simon and Schuster, 1974

Ryan, W., *Blaming the Victim.* New York: Random House (Vintage), 1970

Schillebeeckx, Edward, *The Mission of the Church.* New York: Seabury, 1973

Sider, Ronald J., ed., *The Chicago Declaration.* Carol Stream, Ill.: Creation House, 1974

Soujourners, magazine of the People's Christian Coalition, 1029 Vermont Ave., N.W., Washington, D.C., 20005

Sumner, William Graham, *Folkways.* New York: Dover, 1959

Sweezy, P., and C. Bettleheim, *On the Transition to Socialism.* New York: Monthly Review Press, 1971

Synod of Bishops, *Synodal Document on Justice in the World,* Second General Assembly, Rome, Nov. 30, 1971. Boston: St. Paul Editions, 1971

"The Sixties: Radical Change in American Religion," *Annals of The American Academy of Political and Social Science,* January, 1970

Troeltsch, Ernst, *Social Teachings of the Christian Churches.* New York: Macmillan, 1931

United Nations, "Declaration on the Establishment of a New International Economic Order," United Nations: 3201-VI, May 1, 1974

Vawter, Bruce, "Introduction to Prophetic Literature," *Jerome Biblical Commentary.* Englewood Cliffs, N.J.: Prentice Hall, 1968, I, 223-229

Walter, E. V., "Pauperism and Illth: An Archaeology of Social Policy," *Sociological Analysis,* 34 (Winter, 1973), 239-254

Weber, Max, *The Protestant Ethic and the Spirit of Capitalism.* New York: Chas. Scribner's Sons, 1958

Weber, Max, *The Sociology of Religion.* Boston: Beacon, 1963

Whyte, William H., *The Organization Man.* New York: Doubleday (Anchor), 1957

Wilmore, Gayraud, *Black Religion and Black Radicalism: An Examination of the Black Experience in Religion.* New York: Doubleday (Anchor), 1973

Wilson, Brian, "An Analysis of Sect Development," *American Sociological Review* 24 (1959), 3-15

Wilson, Edward O., *Sociobiology: The New Synthesis.* Cambridge, Mass.: Harvard Univ. Press, 1975

Winter, Gibson, *The Suburban Captivity of the Churches: An Analysis of Protestant Responsibility in the Expanding Metropolis.* New York: Doubleday, 1961

Zaretsky, Irving I., and Mark P. Leone, *Religious Movements in Contemporary America.* Princeton, N.J.: Princeton Univ. Press, 1974